BUST A RHYME

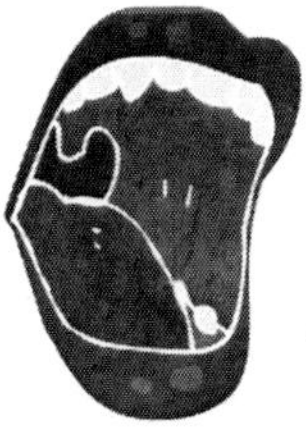

I SHUFFLE THROUGH MY MIND
TO SEE IF I CAN FIND
THE WORDS I LEFT BEHIND
- GREEN DAY

LONDON & THE HOME COUNTIES

Edited By Shariqua Ahmed

First published in Great Britain in 2017 by:

Young Writers
Remus House
Coltsfoot Drive
Peterborough
PE2 9BF
Telephone: 01733 890066
Website: www.youngwriters.co.uk

Book Design by Spencer Hart

SB ISBN 978-1-78820-822-2
Printed and bound in the UK by BookPrintingUK
Website: www.bookprintinguk.com
YB0319FZ

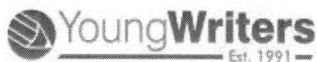

FOREWORD

Welcome, Reader, to 'Busta Rhyme – London & The Home Counties'.

For Young Writers' latest poetry competition, we asked our writers to wow us with their words and bust out their bard side!

The result is this collection of fantastic poetic verse that covers a whole host of different topics.
Get ready to be blown away by these passionate poems about love and relationships, school and bullying, equality and human rights, and demanding day-to-day issues that come with living in today's society. This collection has a poem to suit everyone.

Whereas the majority of our writers chose to express themselves with a free verse style, others gave themselves the challenge of other techniques such as acrostics and rhyming couplets.

There was a great response to this competition which is always nice to see, and the standard of entries was excellent, therefore I'd like to say a big thank you and well done to everyone who entered.

Shariqua Ahmed

CONTENTS

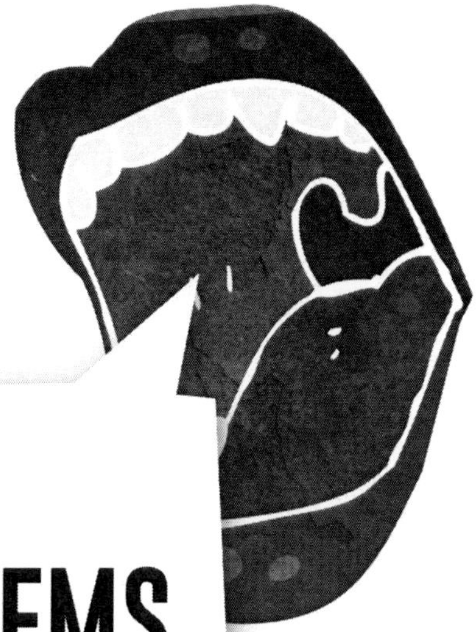

THE POEMS

When The Bomb Dropped

Crawling across the plains and life-filled land
I saw the star - its flash - and acted and
Gripped hope, held tight, bent low, so that I might
Be born like a baby once more: with skin,
But God floods Earth and wipes away all sin,
Then burns the Earth, but all the life within,
Freezes over. The soot blocks out the light
And falls as ash which contains all the might
Of futile life... It settles silently,
Igniting survivors aflame-alight -
While starved scorpions scavenge skeletons
Amongst cockroaches which brawl violently
Over burnt flesh, like those men over cash
Who ended history in man's brief flash.

Cheks Nweze (16)

Gone

John was found dead yesterday.
They said he went peaceful.
It was time, they said.
What do they know?
What does anyone know?
And what does it matter, besides?
Doesn't change the fact,
That he's dead.

The mourners made sure,
His indifferent corpse,
Received the best of treatment.
They said it was the best,
They said it showed respect,
A final place to rest.
And what does it matter, besides?
Doesn't change the fact,
That he's dead.

He lives on in memory, they say,
He's captured in the eternal images of the past,
They say,
They say he lives in our hearts,
It's what he would have wanted.
And what does it matter besides?
Doesn't change the fact,
That he's dead.

And nothing will,
Not ever,
For he has been lost,
As we all will be,
Marked by but a candle,
Till out goes the flame.

This poem is for John,
Small compensation, indeed.
I write it,
To give myself peace.
But what does it matter?
It doesn't change the fact,
That he's gone.

Jacob Potter (13)
Central Foundation Boys' School, London

Refugee

There's always someone standing on their own
Outside the crowd who looks lonely and petrified,
It makes me want to go up to them,
And get their smile back again.

I wonder what it's like to be unwanted and different,
If inside you're the same as everyone else,
It makes me agonised at your pain
And I wish we could swap positions.

I wish I could build a shelter for all,
So you're not stuck in rain and cold.
Anger boils up in me when others just ignore you,
And carry on their lives, like nothing was ever there.

Some people wonder why you are not home,
Warm and snug,
But I completely understand.
Your homeland has been destroyed and I feel bad for you,

I want our world to be a better place.

Grace Lam (11)
City Of London School For Girls, Barbican

First Impressions

The images that spring to mind,
All black and white I seem to find.
Not blue or red or any green,
I know inside it's sad, it seems.

Yet every time,
I seem to try,
To linger, explore or find out,
I found my thoughts all filled with doubt.

Though, one day, I get a hold of myself,
See the book and feel sick at my thoughts.
Jamaia is the owner of this book it read
I soon can't help but lose myself and soon come out with feeling
A thought, it's a deed.

Wandering around all by myself,
'Are you Jamaia? Do you know Jamaia?
More shaking heads until I see a girl
This is black, just like the book,
But soon feel foolish at this thought.

'Are you Jamaia?
You have a friend.'

Mia Roberts (12)
City Of London School For Girls, Barbican

Me

You can't blame me for who I am.
You can't blame me for what I look like.
All you do is break me.

Your hateful words penetrate me,
Deep into my soul.
I know how you judge me behind my back,
I know how you hate my hair,
I know how you hate my skin colour,
I know it all.

But do I care?

No.

I wasn't born to hear your opinion about me.
I have bigger things to think about.

Like my friends
Like my family
Like myself

Me.

Lena Athreya (11)
City Of London School For Girls, Barbican

Diversity

It's not just about what we wear, how we look,
The colour of our skin,
Or the type of food we cook.
There's more to us than what we can see,
What about the feelings we have inside?
Everyone is different in many ways
Wouldn't it be boring to all be the same?
Where have you been?
What's it like?
We are all special,
We live in different places,
Come from all around the world,
We should all be treated the same.
Speaking different languages is a talent,
Not an embarrassment
Embrace it!

Daniella Smilgaitis (11)
City Of London School For Girls, Barbican

Differences

They know you're there
They feel your conscience
Yet they judge you
Like you cannot hear them
Like you do not notice
Like you do not care

Maybe you are different
But what does different really mean?
They blame you for who you are
They tell you who you should be
But you just have a dream
And no one there can stop you.

You are who you want to be
And no one can tear you down.

Saskia Hunter-Thielemann (11)
City Of London School For Girls, Barbican

Difference

The world is filled with difference
Yet ignorance remains
The only thing, the only thing,
Needed for us to come together; acceptance
Weaker sex
Stronger race
Better person
Why?
The world seems a competition
Do we need a winner?
Rules of the world,
Do we need to obey?
First impression:
Stereotypes
Better ways
Why?
We are unique, why change
Now.

Fedra Androulidaki (12)
City Of London School For Girls, Barbican

Am I?

Am I too fat?
Am I too thin?
Am I too ugly?
Are my eyebrows too bushy?
Or are they too thin?
Am I too hairy?
Is my hair too short?
Is my hair too long?
Do my legs show too much?
Are my arms too long?
What else is wrong with me?
Is this what I would tell my younger self?
No...
I am me.
I am perfect just the way I am.

Kobika Dilipkumar (12)
City Of London School For Girls, Barbican

Why Am I Different?

Eyes stare at me.
Thousands.
I wonder why
I'm treated with such hatred
It's not my fault
My face is ugly
Full of scars, deformed.
Standing alone,
Drowning.
In an ocean full of sharks
That kill
I need consoling
I need a friend
That's all I want
All I need.

Khushi Bhalla (12)
City Of London School For Girls, Barbican

Differences Of Hate

We are all different,
You need to understand.
There is no reason to be racist,
There is no need to be bad.

Just because we look different,
Doesn't mean we're insane.
We are still like you,
There is no need to be a pain.

Kaviniy Akilakulasingam (11)
City Of London School For Girls, Barbican

Fire

Fire is an heirloom,
Passed down to us from the first person who created it.
It is a sign of hope
And simultaneously a sign of destruction.
It steals the external life,
Just to keep itself alight.
Yet, it still warms our hearts.

Fire is what brought us together.
Countless hours were spent in front of it.
And with the flow of time,
The door to the future was unlocked,
Which helped us create who we are now.
Fire has enabled the creation of the civilisation and technology.
But as time progresses, the technology
Will destroy the light that initiated us
And our only hope.

Magdalena Sulek
Coombe Girls' School And Sixth Form, New Malden

Rest

I need to get out,
Get out of this place.
My thoughts, they run wild,
My life is a race.

Too many people,
Too many names,
No room for mistakes,
No time for games.

My desk stacked with papers,
My phone always rings.
Life's not about wealth,
But the joy that life brings.

Today's work will be done by tomorrow at best,
But what I truly desire, is a well-deserved rest.

Marika Marathas (12)
Coombe Girls' School And Sixth Form, New Malden

England's Mountain Green

Grey skies, January exercise, our tendency to apologise,
Our red-skinned phone boxes, post boxes, urban foxes,
We love the Royal Family, sarcasm, wit and irony,
Bank holidays, punctuality, 'Terribly sorry!'

Home of cricket, runs and wickets, Oyster cards, tube tickets,
World Cup '66, David Beckham's free kicks, half-time, fish and chips
Premiership, stiff upper lip, banter and quips.
Beer and darts in the pub, barbecues with corn on the cob, tea parties,
Upper-class snobs.

Have you seen the traffic, or the weather? Purple heather, umbrellas,
The Rolling Stones, The Ramones, Abbey and Yellowbrick Road,
British Empire, victorious Navy, roast chicken with OXO gravy,
Canines, felines, queuing in lines, 70s towns, working in the mines.

In amongst the chaotic nation, is beauty quite profound,
Picturesque Yorkshire Moors and green grass on the ground,
Tall towers in our great city, chalky cliffs on Dover's coast
And small country villages enjoying a Sunday roast.

Tom Pullan (14)
Eton College, Windsor

Valerie

I remember the night of Dad's birthday a long while ago
when after the guests had filtered away, Mum lit the fire
and turned the lights off and Grandma sat at the piano
and she trapped the keys with her then delicate fingers,
while we sat there, shivering at those gentle chords.

The elegance of her hunched fingers and those rolling tunes
- a breezy beauty. I think it was Debussy.
The fire cast a sheen - a halo - on her furrowed face.
In her heyday. She didn't have to look at the keys.
In the concerts, they would snap back and forward as
Her eyes fitted across the pages.
And she was jumpy and sprightly,
Now she sits there, a misty, distant wraith that I'm
probably imagining.

At first the words don't hit home to a kid of eight.
Those hollow, meaningless words, it only dawns
when you think about it.
and then it hits.

We got into the car. The black Mercedes-Benz
Barreled into an endless past. The funeral...
Procession. A graceful edgy of loss and legacy.
'Why are people born, Mummy?'

Searing tears, scarlet cheeks,
an irrepressible lump in my throat
and I was the wellspring of anger that suffused
the bathroom.
Squalls of tears.
The cracked mirror and hot liquid down my face, burning,
Boiling, pouring, and I wondered why biological matter must
dwindle into powdery ash and why all the feeling - all the
soul - has to dissipate into thin air and be gone forever.
Why she had to go.
Mummy told me to be quieter
But I wouldn't
I wouldn't
I wouldn't.

'Grandma, where are you, Grandma?'

We stood outside in that hot, sticky, stifling afternoon.
Waiting for that other funeral to finish.
A conveyor belt of loss. Spirals of black smog, strangled
snakes from the cremation. A few hushed
Quips circling - pathetic attempts to lighten the mood.
Stilted small talk.
Gallows humour. Senile strangers gave me
their 'condolences'.
They kept saying how brave she was to the end.
Straggly rainfall.
Mum in the corner steeling herself. Tearless sighs, red eyes.
She went to the bathroom.

But I know that her legacy won't fade into that
Meaningless dust, that you wipe away from the table.
Because she was the hub of the family and the matriarch.
She was the friend. She was the one.

I remember vivid things.
Fishing the board games. Sunday mornings.
Seaside and reading. Reading on the balcony
and bloodshot red seeping
Through the clouds and the spires mottling the horizon, tiny
Harmless knitting needles. A welter of colours, curled up, snug.
By the TV under blankets. The warmth of her live touch and
Glowing smile. She watched Midsomer Murders.
And, of course, there was the piano.

'Grandma, where are you, Grandma!'

In the last year, she was tetchy. Suddenly waspish
And then kind and we were losing her day by day.
Mum always told us to stay polite.

We walked back from the reception. We savoured
Each other's silent company and the comfortable quiet.
The soft, jaundiced lamplight spilled out into the inclement night.
Puddles were burnished, sheets of steel in the moonlight.
Is she up there? Illusory thinking.

I sneaked into her bedroom one night, a few days
Before she left. Sleeping. No garish scars. A pallid
Face; thin cheeks. I remember thinking how they
used to be like fat, cosy marshmallows. That was silly.
Stupid. Young. Innocent. The pinched nose. Those green
eyes.
Her hair combed back like satin curtains to reveal
The blanched forehead. No stench of death blemished
Her. That would come later. then, it was perfume.
White. Like nothing.

And in the few last days, you could see that her conviction
That 'she wouldn't be gone until a long while' was wavering,
Of course, she didn't know that. Death isn't a wilted flower.
There is no flower. Cliches. Death is a shock.
Death doesn't come knocking on your door.
It bangs down the door and knocks over
The furniture and mucks up everything in your life
and daubs the walls with blood.
Death is psychedelic and haunting. Of course, time heals it.
But it burns hot and leaves a brand.

Tonight I stare up at the whitewashed ceiling.
The pure, unsullied ceiling.
I hear mum in the living room.
Not bawling. Quietly.

This time, I
Mutter with her:

'Valerie, where are you, Valerie?'

Simon Billings (14)
Eton College, Windsor

Community Service

Wallpaper peels time, flaking
And swelling inwards away, seething
Against itself in grimaces.

Self-sure clocks regiment the walls,
Workers in supervision, greet the visitors.
Tidying mess, chairs begrudged against
Tables. The effort is appreciated, you know.

The effort you make to keep them comfortable.

The stare seems pregnant, burrowing
Into you and him, refractory,
Demanding a response, but
It's difficult you know, what with
All the life going on, to visit. It stares.

Probing the silence with guilt and torment
And but look at the time, we must
Be off you know, traffic can be a real
Nightmare in this season. Same
Time next month? The clock dribbles,
Smoothening shame while the car pulls
Away, like wallpaper.

Roderick Howland Jackson (17)
Eton College, Windsor

Look Closer

Through the scratched glass of the sky painted window,
In the centre of the kitchen that we all wished was a couple of feet wider,
There is a family and a table, a square table.
Dancing blonde hair tickles eyeballs and their pupils,
While ketchuped lasagne is scooped into smiles and maybe even giggles.
Stories are told and responded to with stories.
Trying to plan Christmas, our Christmas.
Trying to repay our parents
With a painting of their children enjoying the world;
In a way they have forgotten how to do, but not how to feel.
This moment here now.

Look closer,
Foggy pupils dissolve in red-veined eye sockets.
We keep talking with fear of death at stopping,
We keep commenting on how the lasagne is so much better this week,
With fear of looking at each other as human flesh.
Bare, naked and maimed in the wilderness,
Running from shadows.
This is the waiting room for a sorrowful journey
Away from anything as pleasant as the people we think we might be. Maybe.

Look closer,
We shuffle into varnished pews,
We look forward at the hanging prince of peace,
We try to work out if the priest is reusing jokes about John's Gospel.
We look up. We feel we are alone.
The house will be silent for an hour on return.
While we all feel the way eternity stretches beyond us and behind us.
Sitting in our grey rooms, with feathers poking sharp out of the pillows.
We shiver at the thought of it.
Or is it just me?

Look closer,
Blackened mirrors bounce fragments of conversations into every corner.
This, over time, occupies space that really ought to be left alone,
Especially when we have to dig out the nice teapot for our guests.
Sip, 'So then we realised we were in completely the wrong place'
Sip, 'So we all bundled back into the car with our clubber'
Sip, 'And would you believe it, the dog had run off'
Sip, 'But not to worry we made it in the end. My word, this is good cake!

Do I taste almonds?'
Perhaps it won't be like this until I die.
Perhaps mine eyes have seen the glory of the coming of the Lord.
And he comes with far more than lost dogs and... and almonds.

Look closer,
Stop messing around, pay attention.
The neighbours say Father Mathews died slow.
They say they heard the wailing every day around six,
They say some nights it was too much,
They say they began to hate him.
The trains are down from here to London,
We are encouraged to consider, 'Alternative routes over the Christmas period.'
No chance of that,
No, I think the First Great Western pamphlet was used to get the fire started,
Before the front door was locked shut,
Whilst tears land on wrapping paper upstairs.

Frank Baring (17)
Eton College, Windsor

Ants

Mindlessly they charge on,
Battle formations, brothers in arms,
Scuttling, climbing, clambering,
Hopelessly up the slope
Disappear down a hole,
Rows and rows fall away.
Endlessly, mindlessly,
The toll rises.

Hollow, wooden,
They are moved along
Like a playset,
The scene is perfect disorder;
Nothing out of place.
Factory workers under the urging sun,
Monotonously, hollow,
Embracing their oppression.

Onwards, onwards,
Each purposeful in the chaos,
Like a traffic jam without anger
Each must fulfil its duty
Before the time comes,
Neither hate, nor camaraderie.
Onwards. Without thought,
A unit, a single being.

George Baily (13)
Eton College, Windsor

The Perfect Shot

A click, and a flash.
The black metallic body fits perfectly to his hand.
The trigger has been pulled,
The shot has been taken.

One button, that's all.
One button defines everything that you've ever known.
Frozen; or moving, it's all the same.
To the person pulling the trigger.

The light must be right:
Neither too dark, nor too bright.
To be seen, but to be unseen.
The key; to be in the shot.

The grids mark out the victim,
Lined up on the corners.
The framing must be right,
Or the shot will be ruined.

Despair, as the shot didn't work,
Reframe. Refocus.
Blur out the background.
Focus on the person.

The black metallic body is not stable.
'Must set up the mount,' one mutters to themselves.
To shoot straight
You have to be still.

Too quick and you'll miss,
Too slow and you'll miss.
Timing is necessary,
To take the perfect shot.

The target's out of range.
The lens must be changed.
That's better.
Focus, now refocus.

There's red everywhere:
The clothes, the backdrop, the shot.
There are screams from afar,
As the self-timer goes off.

Knowledge turns to focus
And then to anxiety followed finally by relief.
This is the time-lapse of one shot,
From beginning to end.

The artsman smiles to himself.
He got the perfect shot.
It took some time,
But his job is done.

He goes back to his office,
He did what they wanted.
He reviews his shot. The shot.
He could improve that bit here; and that bit there.

He made an impact.
Without him, the shot wouldn't have been taken.
He had to focus and frame
But most importantly; pull the trigger.

As he sits down. Fully trained. Fully equipped. A professional.
A photographer.

Jasper Sodha (14)
Eton College, Windsor

Paper

The weakest, yet the most important,
The skin of life embraces all.
The saviour of some,
The bane of others.
It kills, it saves; it is fate.

The weakest, yet the most important.
It is God. It has life, it has death.
An artist, portraying nature at its best,
It has the life of an explorer,
Travelling from place to place.

The weakest, yet the most important.
As puny as a feather, as vicious as snow.
It will punish, save and perish. It has no emotion.
Worth nothing, yet worth the life of man.

The weakest, yet the most important.

Aryaman Sangwan (14)
Eton College, Windsor

Bermuda

When I was young,
My cradle was an emerald, rolling in the sea.

We slept with the island
The tree-frogs, croaking a soft lullaby
And the salty breeze, gently ruffling our hair.

Delicate sea birds floated above us,
The wild Atlantic winds suddenly
Calm.
Still.
Their songs tumbled down into celebrating reed-flutes, and
The clamour of waves filled the Gombey's
Drums, which pulsed to ancient beats, moved worn-out feet,
Pleased in the morning to smiling, greet.

At sunset the sky was decorated elaborately, painted with lavish strokes of
Deep blue, bold yellow, soft red.
The paint dripped off the canvas above onto the island.
The blue fell into the sea,
The mountainous Atlantic waves, hailing from unfathomable distances,
Carried us like babies.
The gold dropped onto the beaches, onto the sand, where we built
Castles fit for kings, and the next moment,
Crushed them.

The red dripped onto the hibiscus, which stood out delicate and beautiful against the green.
I lived enveloped by colours of
Joy and laughter and adventure
But
Suddenly, I was plucked out of the paint pot, hurried to a new world of grey.
Grey skies over grey seas by grey houses, filled with people with grey personalities.
These days are years, cold, bleak mornings, dragging on and on, time itself drowsy.
You feel
Every
Tick
Of
The
Clock.

But the colours stuck to me, and
I will paint this land with my colours,
Or die trying.

Pennybridge Barn McConachie (14)
Eton College, Windsor

Time Of Day

In the morning, the place I want to be
Is Porto Ercole in Italy.
The calm and quiet of the cove is cracked
By Dad's old motorbike, rusty and red,
Which does the early morning rounds to get
The daily supplies - pizza, fresh figs and bread.

But after lunch, the place I wish I was,
Is Long Island in America.
After work is done the tennis has
Been played, I'm lying in the peaking sun,
Surveying others dodging ten foot waves,
And knowing my freedom has only just begun.

As the day moves on, I am content to rest,
At home in London; evenings are the best.
With homework finished and double checked, I jump
In star formations onto cushions soft
And slump into feathered valley, while
My thoughts of days to come are held aloft.

But at the end of the day, I cannot lie,
I'd rather spend my night in bright Dubai.
The city is still alive when it's dark,
Bustling with cars and luminous from all;
The people dressed in fine, flashy clothes,
Moving around the buildings, which stand tall.

I'm fortunate to have been to these sights,
To experience the vivid views and lights.
But something more precious than souvenirs
That I have brought back home, are memories,
Which fill my mind each time I think of such
Amazing scenes and incredible, wild journeys.

Luca Guerrini-Maraldi (15)
Eton College, Windsor

Sapphire Eyes

Gentle silence, spring-blue light,
Child of a winter's night.
Wrapped and closed eye she sleeps,
In her arms, floating deep.

Growing, growing she crawls,
Soon ignores her mother's calls
Flowing and forming into skies;
Innocent with sapphire eyes.

Step by step. She is almost complete,
Packed with Joy, Love, Deceit.
Frail and shaking on she goes;
Stretching into a morning pose.

Seeking cyan, piercing blue,
Youth and Vigour life renew.
Aura swims and Spirit flies;
Brave and bold with sapphire eyes.

Then the cool and breeze sets in,
Flying kite held by a pin.
Steady, holding, catching air;
Curling strings of swirling hair.

Soon her body starts to taint,
Orange, yellow, salmon paint.
Charring edges fall away,
Consumed by the close of day.

Left to doze and convalesce,
Velvet stars the sky traverse.
In her womb, the seed now lies;
A blue moon girl with sapphire eyes.

John White (14)
Eton College, Windsor

Guerrilla Warfare

Behind each wall,
Behind each smiling face.
The shadow of betrayal,
The doubt of one another.

Each walking man;
Or woman.
You make the choice
On pulling the trigger.

No feelings of kindness,
No generosity.
The sun still rises,
But with one fewer beating heart.

All around
The walls close in.
Fewer places to hide,
Only more to try.

Underneath your laughs,
Your belittling thoughts,
A maze of tunnels,
Intertwining, convoluting.

Promising plans
End in hopeless attempts.
Beaten by those
Who belong to you.

They wound us,
Because we kill them.
We do not understand,
Do not see,

That each drop of blood matters
Less than the drop of their flag.
Each ruined man
Counts as a victory.

Yet each marking on the grave
Lacks a name,
Lacks a hero.

Paris Suksmith (14)
Eton College, Windsor

Breakdown

The wasteland stretches
Off into the horizon,
Grey, deserted.

A rusty, abandoned theme park looking dejected,
Like a loaf of bread moulding;
Once fresh.

The theatres and Ferris wheel;
Now mortuaries,
And silent commemorations of the dead.

The buildings sparkle,
But these are not fireworks,
There are no children looking on, mesmerised,
Only Cyclopean mice and five-legged sheep

who should be pasteurising for eternity,
But there is no grass.

A cement dome covers it,
Blocking out the sun,
The revitaliser.

The dome protects the outside world,
Keeping it safe.

But from what?
Their own mistakes? Their own errors?

A future once so promising;
Now bleak.

Edward Hilditch (14)

Eton College, Windsor

Seagulls

They fly, they rest,
Seagulls darting over our heads,
Soft gusts of wind in a storm.
Their eyes are drills fixed on people
Beside the calm water, crusts of bread in their hands
Waiting to be snatched.
They pounce on humble fish and insignificant insects
Who fear for their lives. The terrifying seagull
Patrols the open air; nothing stops it from ruling.

Harvey Lin (14)
Eton College, Windsor

The Beautiful Game

Football,
The beautiful game,
We all love it, we all play it, we all enjoy it,
We all enjoy it, it's amazing.
I play it, you play, we all play it,
Every boy, every girl, every man, every woman,
Every country.

Clubs, players, legends, fans, managers, trainers;
They all love the beautiful game.

World-class strikers, wingers, midfielders, defenders,
Goalkeepers.

Goalscorers, goalstoppers.
They kick it, yet they worship it.

Past, present, future, brilliance everywhere.

Messi, Ronaldo, Neymar, Pogba, Zlaton,
They play it like their life.
Won, lost, injured, hated,
They've all been through it,
But they had those unforgettable moments,
That we dream to have.

The beautiful game,
We all love it.
Football.

Gurpreet Singh (14)
Featherstone High School, Southall

Hopelessness

I feel so odd, I feel so alone,
I'm too young to take it on my own.
The tears I cried - expressed in this song,
They call me homosexual but is there anything wrong?
It's God's creation, a world where we belong,
I'm too young to take all this stress,
You've made my life a horrible mess.

I'm not saying that I don't fight,
Not for reasons like being unfit, or a short height,
Why bully the people who don't want to fight?
Thinking of the fear, I don't wanna leave my home.
When my mum asks me why,
I act all weird, although I really wanna cry.
You can be nice too, if you give it a try.

All that verbal abuse, it hurts real bad,
Why do you trip me - cos I'm brown, black or white?
Yo, Mr Bully, is it against your right?
You hit me, kick me, bring me to the ground,
I've got bruises all around.
I don't wanna fight, I wanna learn,
All those kicks, they really burn.
My circumstances are low, my life's taking a turn.

I wish I wasn't born,
You might look like a butterfly,
But you sting like a bee,
And you really don't see,
You don't see the pain, the fear, the terror,
I wanna spread my wings, I wanna fly too

Now I'm flesh and blood
Forgive me please.

Isha Sohail (13)
Featherstone High School, Southall

Before You Judge

You get out of bed,
Exhausted and dead.
An hour later you're out of the house,
You walk to the bus stop.
One, there's a lady with a Hijab that's bad
Ten minutes later you're in the shopping centre,
Two, a man in a wheelchair, he's young
And is wasting government money.
Three, a woman sitting in the corner,
Alone, done something wrong.
You didn't think about it, it happened
We all judge people without thinking
It's part of human nature
But, before you judge, take a moment.
The first lady will be your doctor soon,
Bet you didn't know that,
The second man fought for your country,
Risked himself for you.
The third lady has depression
Alone, anxious scared.
People say,
'Don't judge a book by its cover,
When we do it every day.

Wouldn't it be nice if we could live
In a world where people don't have
To hide in threat of people judging them;
That would be nice.
What a lovely place that would be.

Shae Moors (12)
Featherstone High School, Southall

Flowing Deep In Music

The rhythm of the soul,
Where nothing ain't foul,
Music is the way I can flow deep,
My path ain't that steep.
I'll be hitting up the drums,
I don't want you to come,
I'll go on my ones,
While I am slapping my drums.
I don't want no one
Or I'll be:
Trapping,
Rapping,
Slapping,
Your heads off.
Music is the path for me to follow,
If you put me in a box that is hollow,
I'll start:
Rapping,
Trapping,
Slapping,
My way out.
I don't mess about.
When I hit the drums,
I'll be on my ones,
I've been through a lot you see,
I've been through a lot.

From splashing cash,
To getting cash,
I've been through a lot.
Put me in a prison and watch me start:
Slapping,
Rapping,
Tapping,
I'll try to break free.
No prison can hold me.
No one can touch me,
When I'm with my bro,
When I was five I wish I could rap, yooo.

Mithun Someswaran (13)
Featherstone High School, Southall

Love To Each Other

Love,
What is love?

Love is a secret box,
It has good,
It has bad,
It has happiness,
It has sadness,
It has problems,
It has solutions,
But it has love.

What is good happiness?
The fabulous laugh,
The comfort caring,
The romantic feelings,
The lovely time,
But mostly, being together.

What is bad sadness?
The hours waiting,
The yearn, crying,
The worried misunderstanding,
The over-time work,
But mostly the separation.

What are the solutions to problems?
The amazing time to spend together,
The delicious meal to have together,
The fun games to play together,
The loving help to give to each other,
And most importantly the love;
To give, to spend together!

Jaspreet Khaneja (14)
Featherstone High School, Southall

Universe In My Room

Lying in my bed, staring at the ceiling,
It makes me have a good feeling.
When I see the hour glass nebula
I get filled with delight
The stars and constellations shine bright.

The planets make me feel relaxed and right
We look at the stars in the middle of the night.
The sounds of the planets are creepy.
The strange sounds of the planets make me feel elated.

My room is the best,
My room, I adore.
It is great with Gustav Holst playing
Who could ask for more?

The projectors are cool,
I feel good,
With music playing in the background,
I am misunderstood.
Am I in space?

So that ends our poem with planets moving
At a different pace
I hope you have enjoyed it
And remember to think - space.

Amarveer Jandu (11)
Featherstone High School, Southall

Life

Life is happiness, full of joy, like getting married.
Life is sadness, crying over someone's death.
Life is about suffering, not getting time to play.
Life is about enjoying, playing with good friends.
Life teaches you about violence and wars in Syria.
Life teaches you about peace, you get helping someone.
You get love in life, from your family and friends
You get hatred in life, from who are jealous of you
Discovering racism is part of life.
Discovering discrimination is part of life, just because of your belief.
Heartbreaks are what you get in life by people you love.
Crushes are what you get in life, by liking people.
You get reward in life, e.g. getting a phone for your GCSE results.
You get punishment in life, e.g. getting detention for not doing your homework.

Jaspreet Kaur (13)
Featherstone High School, Southall

Mums

For as long as I remember,
You were always by my side;
To give me confidence in my stride.

For as long as I remember,
You were the one I look up to,
So strong, so pretty, so caring.

For as long as I remember,
You were the one I loved, since day one;
Full of laughter, full of love.

For as long as I remember,
And still today,
You're everything a mum should be.

For as long as I remember,
There are no words, that can express how I feel,
You never kept a secret, always stayed real.

For as long as I remember,
You're the one who had an unbreakable bond with me,
And you're the mum you should be!

Manal Ali (12)
Featherstone High School, Southall

Friends Turn To Enemies

When you're at lunch,
They save you a seat,
So I can join them and eat.
I make you happy and jolly,
Then we eat an ice cream lolly.
We start to laugh and celebrate,
That tomorrow is going to be a better day.
We will revise and be friends forever.
When we break up, I'm on my ones,
All my best friends become ex-cones.
So I delete her number,
Then she's calling on plus 44,
Next she's knocking at my door.
You say you're my friend,
I'm keeping up with the lies fam- it's hard for me,
You're not lying, say promise then.
Sometimes I wonder if friends are worth fighting for.
Then I remember your face and I'm ready for war.

Nur-Al-Huda Nur (13)
Featherstone High School, Southall

A Fresh Beginning

To have a fresh beginning,
Wishing for another chance,
Turning away from the path of mistakes,
Turning towards a chance.

To have a fresh beginning,
Changing a chance into a new dawn,
As a new day is here,
Another path arises.

To have a fresh beginning,
To be stuck in the middle,
To turn a wish to reality,
To have to make a choice.

To have a fresh beginning,
Seeing everyone start again,
Making sure that's me next time,
To be enjoying it with my friends.

It's a new day,
A new chance,
A new beginning,
It's an opportunity to dream big,
And to live bigger.

Hudda Mahamud (12)
Featherstone High School, Southall

Soldier

March down the headquarters,
Fire down the enemy.
Sergeant knows the code,
March it down the road.

The boss is on his way,
The reward could help me play,
But... the enemy is still there,
Scared, petrified, horrified, confused,
The armour on my body gives me confidence
The bulletproof helmet gives me trust.

You're lucky you're not a soldier,
If you were, trust me you would get
Flashbacks every day.

The enemy still on their way;
Bullets flash past.
I take a deep breath, start firing,
Soon it was over
I know shell shock will happen, fear
It was constant.

Satkaran Singh (13)
Featherstone High School, Southall

Busta Rhyme

Football! Football! Football!
Things good about football are:
Curlers!
Bangers!
Knuckleballers!
Transfers!
Headers!
Corners!
And goals!
Goals! Goals! Goals!
What more to say than goals!

In football you need:
Coordination,
Celebrations,
Passing,
Dribbling,
Don't get warnings,
And skills
Skills! Skills! Skills!
What more to say than skills!

For example:
Scorpion kicks,
Rainbow kicks,
And Teccas
Teccas! Teccas! Teccas!

Ronaldo chop
People that drop
And Messi
The best footballer in the world.

Gabriel Waddi Michael Anthony Koussa (12)
Featherstone High School, Southall

School

School is important,
To our education,
To our instruction,
To our learning,
Because school:
Helps us to have good training,
So in the future we could go to a university,
And have a fine job.
Without school,
We won't have a happy life,
And in the future we could be struggling to live.
School helps us to socialise,
With friends, teachers, people,
The best teachers are those who show you where to see,
And not what to see,
School helps you to manage yourself,
And get over life's problems.
When you start school,
You start it as a seed,
And you leave it as a matured apple.

Bushra Mohamed Isfahan (14)
Featherstone High School, Southall

Life's Not Easy

My life was not easy,
I saw people come and go like a Frisbee.
Back in the day, my mum had no change in her purse,
But still found ways to raise me.
I have no dad, she is a single mum
It's no joke when you are broke
And you're living off crumbs.
Man, it really gets dark in the slums.
Then they took my uncle away, 'cause
They caught him selling some stuff;
But he could never get enough.
Now they knew how much we were struggling
And then the rent's started doubling.
We just needed some help,
To survive and strive
Just for one more day.

Jotham Afonso (14)
Featherstone High School, Southall

Life

Life is the most precious thing
There are two ways in life
Good and bad
Your life, your choice.
Your present is the future.

You complaining for a new Smart phone.
When children in Syria die.
You're fussing about food
While children starve.
You're wondering when the Wi-Fi is on,
While children are wondering if they're
Going to live another day.

You donate to charity.
But if charity is cold like your heart;
Don't you think you should change?

Prabdeep Sidhu (11)
Featherstone High School, Southall

A Perfect World

A world with no hate,
Full of peace and love.
A world with fate,
No negativity towards these above.

A world with no problems,
All children allowed education,
A world with no war,
No violence, just peace.

A world with no tags,
No names, no title.
A world running on positivity
Everyone is allowed their own opinion.

A world with no racism,
A world with no hate,
A perfect world.
But that's just my dream...

Prethty Maniwannan (12)
Featherstone High School, Southall

Food

Food; it changes your mood,
From sad to happy
And makes your day
And makes you want to have your say;
About where to eat,
And on which seat.
Where to have your chicken nuggets,
Maybe go to fast food shops
Feeding many ducks.
Forget that line, I ain't going to give any ducks my Starbucks
Or maybe buy some chocolate
Mmm, tasty.
Stop eating, it's very hasty
My chocolate is very good
Just like food
Food, it changes your mood.

Afsha Tufail (12)
Featherstone High School, Southall

Life, Life

It is like a boy,
Stepping on a toy,
Eating a whole basket of joy.

Also like sitting at home,
Listening to tones,
When your siblings moan.

When your teacher's in a mood,
When your siblings watch cartoons;
In the afternoon.

Also like doing your education,
When your friends have a relation,
To your nation.

Like doing English, science and maths,
Like the best in the match.

Hamza Ahmed Omar (11)
Featherstone High School, Southall

Stop Hating Muslims

So sick to death of always being judged by
The colour of our skins, alone making us as criminals.
Leading you to believe,
Painful, hurtful lies,
Lies that rip and tear apart, the very fabric of our
Once-loving community.
Turning the world against us,
One by one,
We come forward
Begging and saying we are Muslims, not terrorists
Pleading to understand why
Why do some people lie and say
All Muslims are terrorists?

Nafiza Rahman (12)
Featherstone High School, Southall

Art

Art, art, art!
All the colours, bright and dark!
Something close to my heart
Is art!

Yellow, blue, green and pink
Let me think,
Lines, shapes and texture,
Different colours of mixture.

Art is your emotions,
Flowing in a river of imaginations.
Art has the power to inspire,
It also has the power to motivate,
Art, art, art!
Oh! What a wonderful art!

Deandra Fernandes (11)
Featherstone High School, Southall

Poor Life

I'm a child,
Living in a poor family,
Living in a broken house,
With a broken window,
With a broken door,
And a broken heart.
My friends have a PlayStation.
I don't even have a toy car to play with,
How is it fair when others have
More money,
More happiness,
More time,
And more success?
In a world full of inequality
It is difficult to thrive.

Manjot Singh (13)
Featherstone High School, Southall

Become Something

I have ambitions, big ambitions
I have expectations, great expectations
I want to get somewhere in life
I want to make you proud
I want to make you smile
But it wasn't good enough,
All I want is to become something
But to become something, I need to study,
To study I need to learn,
To learn I need to behave,
To behave I need to respect
And to respect?

Karandeep Singh (14)
Featherstone High School, Southall

Sports

Sports, ah sports,
Very healthy and regular.
Sports can be different from each other.
Like football, cricket, Frisbee and hockey,
All different.
Sport is active and has an order.
But my favourite is cricket.
It's very catchy and batty
And very hard to win
But very easy to lose though,
Sport is my life
And cricket is my soul.

Junaid Safi (11)
Featherstone High School, Southall

Love

Love, love
Love hate
Love people
Love fate.

Love heartbreak,
Love education,
Love school,
Love information.

Love is hope,
Love is joy,
Love is imagination,
Love can be with a girl or a boy.

Love life,
Live, love,
Because love is life
And life is love.

Suhaylah Muhammad (13)
Featherstone High School, Southall

Indian Food

Indian foods are followed by Indian culture and festivals.
They are traditional, holy and healthy
Also, they are delicious and mouthwatering
From the twenty-eight states of India.

Butter chicken which is known as 'murgh mahal'
Smells so aromatic and fulfilling that it reaches to Taj Mahal
The amazing sweet, mesmerising tamil Pongal
Made in the beautiful Savitri's Jungle.

The orange, twisted noodle called Jalebi
Dipped in the sugary syrup with a lovely, chewy substance
A pork bhatia shared with a beef pasta
And Revolver Rita enjoys an amazing meat samosa.

Deep fried Chicken 65, causing my taste buds to try
When it arrives; I felt that I was the chicken on that plate
A sweet rice pudding with cashew nuts and golden sultanas
It is the payasam, the sweet, tamil nadu

The sweet, round doughnut dipped in golden syrup
Brown, round, shiny and garnished with dried nuts
The powerful, elegant Rani loves drinking the
Spectacular juice called Nimbu Pani

Madurai's Jigarthanda is the best slushy
It give you joy with healthy organisms
The interminable cone-shaped kulfi, it's so attractive that
It's the true taste of India.

Paneer pizza from the lovely Indian cottage cheese
Peppers, jalapeños, sweetcorn, and the lovely essence of paprika
Aloo gobi, the mixture of fresh cauliflowers with big potatoes
Caja is the best, largest sweet in West Bengal's history.

In food, there are intricate tastes which changes the food to healthy and amazing.

Aswath Diwakaran (12)
Greenshaw High School, Sutton

Imprisoned

I am a girl.
It doesn't matter if I'm black, Christian or straight,
I'm still vulnerable, weak and dependent.
Even though I'm as precious as a pearl,
I'm a fool's bait.

Was I born to feel protected and respected?
Or was I born to feel controlled and submissive?
Can't I dress the way I want and not be judged?
Being female doesn't make me permissive.

I am a guy.
It doesn't matter if I'm white, Jewish or bi,
I'm still told I shouldn't cry.
Because it would make me more sensitive is the reason why.

Why do I have to be aggressive and in control?
Does asking for help really make me less 'macho'?
Or is it just because society believes I have the main role?
Why can't I simply say no?

We live in the 21st century,
Shouldn't this episode be over?
Is this inequality really necessary?
Until then, none of us will be entirely happy being a him or her.

We should be free to feel imprisoned no more.

Alison Afanou (13)
Greenshaw High School, Sutton

Alone

It happened again,
She's alone again,
She really thought it would work this time.
Maybe it's her fate, her destiny,
Maybe it'll be like this forever,
What she wishes for may never come.

She goes unnoticed,
She sits silently,
But someone sees her differently.
Someone like her,
Yet still so unique,
It was a friendship destined to happen.

What once was sadness, became joy.
What once was silence, became laughter.
When something got her down, someone cheered her up.
She found what she'd been looking for;
Care, kindness and understanding,
She was alone no longer.

Ashleigh Prior (14)
Greenshaw High School, Sutton

Untitled

I don't understand why someone would choose to sever the skin of another.
Instead of investing their time in increasing the pride of their mother.
Why would someone choose to end lives
Knowing they're placing one million tears in their mother's eyes?
Why having blood on your hands, earning you respect in the streets?
And to have 'heart' your soul must be filled with lies and deceit,
This is not a poem, but a letter of complaint,
Because seeing youth die is less entertaining than the drying of paint.
I'm trying my best to be the calmest of calm,
But there's too many of us bragging about straps in our palms,
So no, this is not a poem,
These are all facts;
I've been to twenty-four funerals last year and I'm struggling to keep my head intact.
In fact, I don't want to see any more die,
Because truly, I've had enough of having to cry.
I'm tired of having to do anger management and counselling.
And I'm tired of them thinking violence and gang culture and offsprings of single parent housing.

We're only like this because we don't know the truth,
And that's because you keep information from the youth.
Red puddles of past dreams and past experiences,
I'm trying so hard to tell you how it really is.
But it's hard for me to do that, when I'm just a pundit.
Trap music spreads stupidity but other youth still finds it.
And I guess I'm a hypocrite because I have the same music download on my phone.
But I, unlike the youth, know where I want my future to go,
And so;
A formal thought to leave you with,
If you were the youth, would you like the way you live?

Ruth Edwards
Harris Academy Battersea, London

What Do You Do?

What do you do when they come for you?
Do you run? Do you hide? Do you scream or cry?
Do you laugh? Do you smile? Do you forget for a while
That they know what you're thinking? They know what you're feeling.
They know what they'll do when they come for you.

What do you do when they're speaking 'bout you?
Do you join in the fun, once it's all begun,
Or do you turn it away, leave for another day?
This thing leaves you weeping,
'Cause it's keeping you from sleeping,
Which makes your heart start bleeding.
So what do you do when they're speaking 'bout you?

What do you do when they forget 'bout you?
Do you regret what you said?
Do you let them cram ideas into your head?
That you're worthless, you're stupid,
You're just a little kid,
That doesn't know wrong from right,
Don't know how to fight.
Maybe one day it'll just evaporate,
But it won't
So what do you do when they forget about you?

What do *they* do when you come though?
'Cause you start to fight with all your might,
They know that they are wrong,
They know that you're right.
'Cause they can't seem to apologise;
That they made you cry.
So what do they do when you come through?

Kelsey Rorison (13)
Harris Academy Battersea, London

Dad

You never said goodbye
I don't remember you singing me a lullaby.
When I asked about you, she pointed at the sky
And said you had wings and said you could fly.
I would never cry or shed a tear,
For I knew you were always near.

Then, in fierce words and heated fury
The truth became executioner, judge and jury
Its heavy weight broke through the lie
And I learned how you chose to die.
A death so militant, so brutal
I try to erase the image from my mind - it's futile.

I would've wished for you a gentle end
For someone to a hand extend
To roll out on the waves of a dream
That softly wash onto the shores of oblivion - serene.
What reasons for your choice could there have been?
What truth still eludes - unseen?

I know now you could not cope
You felt as if you had no hope
But was I not enough for you to stay?
To save your soul from decay?
Has your soul found the peace it so longed for
Or does it still search for paradise's pearlescent door?

These questions leave me depressed
In limbo, a dishevelled mess
For now I have one parent less
No father, only a father figure
A pain in my heart growing bigger
I'm told to respect your wishes.
But what about my wishes? I was your daughter.

Aliyyah Heynen Singh (13)
Harris Academy Battersea, London

Happiness

They stand in the corner whispering lies,
All I can see is darting eyes
Everything inside me is full of despise
But all I want to do is cry,
On someone's shoulder who really cares,
But no one does, it's just not fair.
I hold it back and walk past them,
Like Heaven or Hell it never ends.
The hate, the anger, the dread and the fear,
Building inside me; year after year.
They seem to think I cannot hear,
As if I'm missing both my ears.
But I'm not -
And it hurts,
And it hurts me deep inside.
I want to hide,
And wait for it to go away
But it won't no it won't
'Cause it happened yesterday and it happened today,
Tomorrow, the next, the day after next
Until I feel like I'm in a wreck and start to cry
As something deep inside, is gone,
Like that care for those people.
Who turned me upside down, around and around,
Back and forth, South and North, East and West.
Like the rest, they hurt like me.

So I stop and I smile
And I leave it all behind me
'Cause the things I have in my life,
Like a bed and a roof over my head
I realise, my life,
It ain't that bad at all
So I go to school and smile like a fool,
Until they go away
And today, well today
I am very happy today!

Deia Thomas (13)
Harris Academy Battersea, London

Heartbreak And Heartache

Why do people love if they know it's going to hurt?
It's just not worth all of the pain.
Obviously relationships are just not at all the same.

There's no point in trying, helping if you can't do it,
Because all the blame will be pinned on you
and you'll feel as if you can't make it.
Just keep yourself to yourself and don't even try to fit.

Relationships are a mad type of reality,
That if you can't understand, it's not really handy,
But if you have the brains and patience by all means, take it on.

If you're in a relationship, then there's no point in saying 'I' or 'me'
Because you both are supposed to go with each other,
Go hand in hand so together you're called 'we'.

For now we can leave relationships and concentrate on the meaning of life,
Doesn't mean wife or husband to be quite right,
It just means to live right,

Once one relationship is over and done with, and you feel as if your free, another person comes along.
That's when you have to be strong and show them the strong individual your parents made you to be.

Jevanna Daniella Grace Princess Sapphire Roberts (13)
Harris Academy Battersea, London

People's Opinion

Many people have different opinions
From different cultures and religion
Opinions about white vs black
Why do you react?
If that person isn't you, then keep your opinion to yourself.
For the same of other people's emotional health.
I was walking to school the other day
There were some boys in the alleyway
The boy just wanted to have some fun and play
There were two from America
And one from India.
The two boys picked on him because he spoke his own language
They pushed him down and attacked him
One of the boys said go back to your country
This left him confused and happy.
Gay relationships, why are people against them?
People want to make them feel hurt and offended
When there's nothing wrong with the same sex in a relationship.
I want you to leave with this thought in mind
Gay, black, white, different religion;
All these people are just fine
So like I said before...
If that person isn't you, then keep your opinion to yourself;
For the sake of other people's emotional health.

Dames Stewart Desir
Harris Academy Battersea, London

I'm Too...

I'm too shy to walk,
Too shy to talk,
I'm too tired to wake up,
Too tired to go to school.

But then again
Who said they cared.

I'm too quiet to speak up,
Too quiet to be noticed,
I'm too impatient to wait,
Too impatient to loiter.

But like I said,
Who thinks they care.

I'm too blind to see,
Too blind to care,
I'm too scared; so I lie,
Too scared to die.

But with the people today,
Who believed they cared.

I'm too religious to have envy
Too religious to detest
I'm too mature to be trifling,
Too mature to complain.

But with this generation,
I know they don't care.

I'm too young and I'm too innocent,
Too young to give consent,
I'm too weird to be the same,
Too weird to be as tame.

But who said they had to care,
And even if they did, it would be rare.
It doesn't really matter, not even to a bee,
Because the only person it matters to is me.

Mariam Abdow (12)
Harris Academy Battersea, London

I Miss You

I miss you,
I still can't believe you're gone,
All the moments we had together,
Everything we had in the past, will always be in my heart,
I still remember when you used to make up nicknames for me,
The way your smile always grew bigger when you saw us,
The way your eyes always shone when you looked at her,
You made me a stronger person,
I've learnt so many things with you,
You told me to fight for my dreams,
You taught me to never give up on things and people I love,
I appreciate you for everything that you have done for me,
You were always there when I needed you,
You were always there when I missed you,
Now that you are gone, I feel so empty inside,
Sometimes I stare into space,
Thinking about all the memories we had,
I sometimes wonder what would have happened if you were still here,
I miss you
Everyone misses you,
There is only one thing I hope,

I hope to see you again,
Just in a different place,
A better place,
See you soon,
I miss you.

Beatrix Cardoso Rodrigues (13)
Harris Academy Battersea, London

Society

What is this pathetic excuse we call society,
Where every time I go on Instagram I hear RIP.
Twelve-years-olds holding knives,
Thinking it's okay to take another person's life.

Girls out here falling for boys,
Who are treating them like unwanted toys.
They put that aside and say, 'But he loves me,'
No darling; he's using you for money.

I'm not here to criticise or tell lies,
I'm here simply because I can't stand another tear.
Coming from a mother's eyes, who just lost her son,
Or a girl who's thinking I wasn't the one.

I know I'm only thirteen,
But I have a dream.
A dream that we put down the knives,
And start saving lives.
That girls learn to love themselves,
And don't have the need to depend on someone else.

That's my dream
And hopefully one day, I can be proud and say this is my society.

Fatima Hersi (13)
Harris Academy Battersea, London

Untitled

I run from the names and the pain.
This Earth is a place, I do not want to remain
In my heart there is a strain.
I try to run away from this pain,
I'm slowly starting to float away
As I hear a voice in my brain screaming, 'Go away!'

Every day I feel this pain,
It's like a train crashing into my brain.
All I ever feel is pain
Waking up every day,
Dreading this school day,
'Go away!' that's all they ever say.

My heart is full of despair
All they ever do is laugh and stare
They never really cared
Negativity is all they ever shared
They may think that they make me scared
But I really don't care.

They really think that it affects me
They need to learn, the true word of respect
It just reflects their personality
Their brains must have wandered
Out of reality.

Tayan Monteiro (13)
Harris Academy Battersea, London

True Love

From the day I met you, I knew you were bad,
From the day I met you, you were scared and sad.
I don't know why I let you into my life,
I don't know why you killed my wife,
I was blind not to see your true self,
Now I have problems with my health,
Depression, anger, pain,
You killed her, all for your gain,
Me and her, we loved each other,
Didn't you think you were killing one's wife, one's sister, one's true lover?
I don't know why you did what you did,
How can I tell my kids? Will I lie?
Just tell them their mother died,
Or will I tell them the truth;
Their mother was killed by a brute.
You deserve more than just prison for life,
Why did you use that knife?
Don't start apologising, don't waste your breath,
The least you deserve is death.

David Asah
Harris Academy Battersea, London

You

You were always nice,
And we had the same eyes.
You came to me when I needed help,
You came at night,
And kissed me like I was a brave knight.
Who always wants to fight!

You cooked me food,
When I was not in the mood,
You told me stories, that I loved,
And I'll always keep it in my heart,
Where I store all my memories,
With you and me, with you and me!

But now I will never meet you again
As you're down underground,
With flowers by your side.
I think about you with my large mind.
24/7, day and night, all year round
And you made lovely sounds
That I'll listen to... all... year... round!

You, you, you,
You, you, you!

Osman Macit (13)
Harris Academy Battersea, London

Different

Because there's no harm in being different
Diversity in looks makes our society;
A place of less anxiety.

To know that I'm not identical to any of you is great,
But many people, they still receive hate;
In countries further away from you or I.

Where, (unbelievably) plastic surgery is seen;
As a gateway to happiness, a good job and a prosperous life.

Where Eurocentric beauty values are valued like
Straight hair,
And skin so fair,
We should all have our own flair.

I just don't want to be trapped in a bubble of your hate.

We're all snowflakes;
Not a single one of us the same
So let's not aim for perfection.

Maida Abdullahi
Harris Academy Battersea, London

Untitled

There wasn't a day when you weren't on my mind,
There wasn't a day where you weren't by my side.
With your crazy personality that drives me head over heels;
Your glistening eyes that I always dream into.
Your perfect smile and that cute laugh...
You make me feel so uplifted and happy.
The day that I saw you in your crib, all tucked up
And cute, I already fell in love with you,
You're so perfect and amazing,
I always thank God for this blessing.
You're a gift from Heaven, my angel that I always want to hold
And never let go...
I will always love you, forever and more.
You may be a little bit annoying, but don't forget that I will cherish you always.

Rachel Nicole Charran (12)
Harris Academy Battersea, London

Racism

Racism, racism is horrible, it shouldn't even be possible.
Alone, taken away for a frown,
Black, white and mixed-race face,
This is their face so deal with their race.
A boy
Sits in the corner, dying, crying,
He's black, so people walk back.
'Please help, I'm dying,' they're lying;
Saying they're coming back
But because he's black, they won't care.
He can't even bare to stare,
Eyes softly closing, he floats in the sky,
Tonight he dies.
Another funeral because of race,
Another family cried,
As their brother, cousin, uncle died.
Because of hate;
It's his fate.

Don't be the person to do this.

Shanaya Millwood (11)
Harris Academy Battersea, London

Untitled

The day I saw you at the hospital, my eyes glistened;
A sparkle of joy was in them.
You were the most beautiful thing I ever saw in my life,
Nine months later and you're still so precious.
Every time I see you, I feel so happy,
You make my day with that big smile on your face.
Your cute giggling and joyous laughs,
I feel so proud to see you grow.
To know you're younger than me and I can always take care of you.
When I hold you, you're so small, you jump up and down.
Day by day you get bigger, oh my, oh my, how the time has flown by...
It's been a year since you were born;
In two months, you'll be one and I can't wait to see you grow.

Alyssa Simone (12)
Harris Academy Battersea, London

Untitled

On the day you passed away
You left your chair and you were trying
To say that no one will replace the day
And everything will be okay.

You left us drowning in our tears,
Hope you're up there drinking beers
And looking down on us trying to say everything will be okay.

Waking up in the morning,
Knowing that you're not in there, snoring.
This is why the house is so boring,
Without you.

Sitting in my bed remembering what you said, that
You're looking down on us, trying to
Say that everything will be okay.

Yasmin Parsons (13)
Harris Academy Battersea, London

Skin Colour

White and black skin are just colours,
Not rich and poor,
Owner and slave,
Or homeowner and homeless,
They're just ordinary colours.

So whether you're black or white,
There is no difference as everyone is equal
If you're black, you're not a slave.
If you're white, you're not bad
So black and white are just colours.

Zakariya Mohamud (13)
Harris Academy Battersea, London

Awakening

Hopes and dreams are stars that seem
Infinitely immune to the distortions of reality.
And in their proximity in space, they are surrounded by gold -
But not gold because gold can melt a mould,
And can disappear - when all they are near
Is stronger than the covalent bonds in diamond.
You cannot mine them with pickaxes: there are no tools;
And the fools who think they are fathomable in our mortal plane
Know little and less every day.
A dream is a fixation, a destination:
Your goal that keeps the demons from devouring your soul.
It cannot be touched,
Not even by you: your imagination's the only link, your subconscious, the only train
To take you from the harsh whips that lash against your skin,
To that blissful feeling you sink in,
And crave the end of every day, so that this fantasy can be yours.
You need the edges of the fairy tales, you need the true love's kiss and 'happily ever after'.
But it all starts with a 'once upon a time', and this is not a vague, unnamed time:
Your time has numbers and dates and letters,
Years and months and days and seconds;

You are dated, as if by carbon, and the dreams you will to be yours,
That you climb ladder after ladder hoping to reach,
Are yours to keep but not yours to live.
Dreams are distortions of reality,
And the reality you aim to live can only be achievable.
You should believe in a destiny that you forge through courage and passion:
A future built on sweat and determination.
Dreams are for those who have no future to create;
It's for those who are lost, and therefore have to make
A life within their mind,
Out of time,
Out of space.
But this is your time: your body, your mind,
To live as if it were a dream dreamt by one who is fixated on the qualities you possess.
No more.
No less.

Sarah Cosgrove (17)
Harris Westminster Sixth Form, London

The Beginning Of The End

'Our motto is, when they go low we go high,' - Michelle Obama

The race got underway,
It was now time for twenty-one to walk away.
It had now come to the final two,
Red vs Blue.
Words and comments had been exchanged
And in the end one side would be ashamed.

I'm with her,
They were all saying
They thought that this election would be easy, a pushover
Despite the orange one saying
It would be unfair.
Not that she was great either,
But most preferred her rather;
Than the man with crazy hair.

Ha ha, a joke he was called,
Thinking that he could build a wall
For Christ's sake, what a fool
The only wall there is,
Is between his head and reality,
And what people did not know, was that they were in for a fatality.

Bang! The election clock is ticking,
The orangutan is winning
Reading messages, saying no
As this country may reach an all-time low.
Half of America is sobbing,
While everyone else's hearts are throbbing.
As he pulled in Michigan, Ohio, Wisconsin,
Her chances went a runnin'

As the election comes to an end,
My mind starts to bend
As I have rage held inside me
As I thought it would've been she, who would guide this country to glory
But, instead, it is a man who makes me worry.
And so now the time has come, to hold our hands together as nations as one
And pray for the world, that we live in peace 'n' harmony
And all I can say is America, I'm sorry.

Elias Daryani (12)
Homefield Preparatory School, Sutton

Coco

My pet, the ferocious cat, Coco,
A guard 'round my house to and fro,
A radar of death with potent sight,
A sharp and bloody bite!

No survivors she leaves, smaller than her,
Stroke her crown and you hear her purr,
Her pride-filled face of secret death,
Her decaying rodent breath.

Always alert, her whiskers twitching,
Her intimidating glare bewitching,
Any mouse who trespasses, it surely dies,
While the others wave silent goodbyes.

And yet she still looks for more daring prey,
She can't let her guard down; she has to stay,
In the house of the Wiggerts, to and fro,
My ferocious loyal cat, Coco...

Jackson Wiggert (11)
Homefield Preparatory School, Sutton

Ban

He hates me but likes you.
What do I do? Do I
Protest? Or face the ban.
We didn't do anything, but he thinks we will.
Do we admit defeat or carry on?
Does it matter if it is fair?
Or should we sit around and not care?
No matter what we do he will not care.

Is it because I worship someone
Other than him? Or because I
Help people, unlike him.
Or because I am kind to people he hates.
He hates me but likes you.
What will you do?

Ayyub Mahbub Gani (12)
Homefield Preparatory School, Sutton

High Hopes

He loved me,
Didn't you,
You know I loved you too.
I was just a prize,
I was nothing to you, under all the lies.
The alcohol you gave me was just to see the difference in me,
Well now I know what I never used to see.
You made me; so I weakened and was defenceless,
Now you have been caught, so do your sentence.
The lies you said,
I just want to be dead.
The feelings I had for you,
You made me think you had them for me too.
I knew my dad would disagree,
The thing is, he's tried to make me avoid boyfriends since I was let free.
Not feeling trapped in the bubble of mistakes,
Is that all it takes, because now I know, you are all fakes.
Compliments are all lies, now I hurt,
You really know how to make a kid feel like dirt.
Why did I get into that front seat,
It's nearly over now, time to defeat.
How many other girls did you do it to?
How would you feel in our shoe
I hope you feel sad.

Because now I know what you've done was bad.
He loved me, didn't you,
You know I loved you too.

Alicia Weeks
Hope Service (PRU), Epsom

Significance

We are all special in our own way,
Doesn't matter what things we say,
How we walk the walk,
Or talk the talk.

We're all special in our uniqueness,
I just have full faith in this,
That anyone no matter who they are,
If they are here or from afar,
That one very special day,
That they could make the world go a different way,
To conceal our future,
Or to suture,
They are very special in their own special way.

No one is the same,
It'll make me insane,
If I see some not how they are,
I will tell that miserable fart,
To be who they are,
Not who they aren't.

We're like a cornflake,
It'll make me shake,
Someone to be who they are,
Not who they aren't,

We can make the world a better place,
Or to make a trace,
To make a brew,
Or to make the new.

Treat everyone how you want to be treated,
Because we were created,
To make this world,
Not like eWorld.

We're just species,
Not made by Mitsubishi,
We are all unique,
From people who like antiques,
To people who like Japanese,
Or who like Chinese,
We are special,
And we are all just precious.

Ayden Carver (12)
Kennet School, Thatcham

Our Change To The World

The world has become something I don't want to live in,
Tormented by us, like being stabbed with a pin.
Bleeding all sorts of equality and kindness,
Covering the world in a thick film of blindness.

Unaware of what is happening all over the place,
Discrimination of gender, religion and race.
Ratings are more important than the truth,
We build twice as many prisons as we do schools.

Our economy is slipping,
As we slowly find our feet.
Throughout the conflict and division,
We are at the edge of defeat.

We have every technology that we ever need,
The average person watches five hours of TV,
We are surrounded by processed and artificial things,
Now marriage is based just over a ring.

Inequality is becoming more and more recognisable
With a life for the rich being one that is advisable.
The ocean life is wearing more and more thin,
For people not managing to find a bin?

The world has become something I don't want to live in,
Tormented by us, like being stabbed with a pin.
Bleeding all sorts of equality and kindness,
Covering the world in a thick film of blindness.

Georgia Jones (13)
Kennet School, Thatcham

We Can Make Their Lives Better

Have you ever wondered about how lucky we are,
When some people in Gambia have not tasted a chocolate bar?
We spend money on things we don't need,
Whilst all some people in Gambia can do is plead.

Whilst we are shoving junk food down our throats,
Some people in Gambia are satisfied with oats.
Don't even get me started on the dirty water,
Whilst some people here in Britain moan about who is shorter.

Their hand-made homes made of water and mud,
What are they to do if there is a flood?
Everything they know would be destroyed or wrecked,
This would cause a devastating effect.

The young children skinny as twigs,
Probably never even heard of figs.
All that they may be used to eating,
Is rice sat on no ordinary seating.

Flu or even chickenpox, they wouldn't stand a chance,
But for us here in Britain, we could soon be back to dance.
We can help these poor people; I am not being funny,
All we need to do is raise a little money.

So what are you waiting for, don't bother writing a letter,
If we all work together we can make their lives better!

Emma Harrison (13)
Kennet School, Thatcham

The Beach

The waves crashing at the shore,
so elegant and serene.
Whilst excited and playful children
rub in their sun cream.

Oh, how I love the beach,
and all the beauties that it boasts;
that can be viewed closely,
using paddle boats.

Let's not forget the wildlife,
that leaves you in awe;
crabs, starfish,
and dolphins galore.

When the pier fills with families,
in the midst of their holidays;
you know the sunset's about to begin,
leaving all who see it in a gaze.

The purples and the pinks,
with the yellows seeping through;
accompanied by the glistening sea,
and a perfect face-on view.

Oh, how I love the beach,
with the euphoria I get
when I suddenly realise
that this conclusion is met.

The beach is made for so much more
than soaking up the sun;
It's where your biggest dreams come true,
through the influence of fun.

That's why the beach is important,
and means something to me;
as I love the relaxing feeling,
of sun, sand and sea.

Andrew McCabe (13)
Kennet School, Thatcham

Away With The Animals

Around the corner the camp axe lies,
Awaiting the gaze of a lumberjack's eyes.
Long forgotten,
All but rotten.
Its sole purpose was rather clever,
To chop down many trees all together.
It often saw a lot of action,
Trying to provide even a fraction,
Of the big fat businessmen's money.
Whilst the wildlife that lived there,
Kept going hungry.
They often said it had to be done,
But would you agree if you were their mum?
The animals only wanted a home,
But now all they can do is grunt and groan.
How about the rainforest stays?
To give the animals, longer days.
Nobody even thinks about animal wellbeing,
The damage caused is practically stealing.
Do you really need that expensive wood table,
If it meant the animal population was certainly not stable.
Next time spare a little thought,
For the damage caused by that luxury you sought.

Adam Hodgkinson (13)
Kennet School, Thatcham

Inequality

Everyone should be equal, we've all got skin and bones,
But there is inequality because of different skin tones,
People get made fun of, it happens every day,
Even in the workplace where they don't get as much pay.

Men and women should be treated the same,
But no, there's sexism which is so lame.
Men think that they are the best and so do women too,
And this is millions, not only a few.

Disabilities are not people's choices or fault,
They would love to run like Usain Bolt.
But instead, they are made fun of and called a name,
All they really want is for people to treat them the same.

Are you one of these people, a victim or a predator?
Don't just watch and be a spectator.
Go out and make the world a better place,
By tackling inequality face-to-face.

Grace Steele (13)
Kennet School, Thatcham

Animal Survival

There are so many animals that just won't survive,
I'm sorry to say that they won't stay alive...
The snow leopard is one; it will eventually die out,
especially with poachers lurking about.

Then there's the polar bear; sad and alone,
on the ice caps, melting in a danger zone.
They are endangered because of their coat,
let's not wear fur, just so you can gloat.

Now the mountain gorilla is a very sad tale,
just so the poachers can put up food for sale.
Living in the jungle, their habitat wrecked,
give some money and show some respect.

Also the black rhino won't survive for long,
why do we do this? It's all going wrong.
There is no reason why we love to kill,
don't be a poacher, just relax and chill.

Joe Morris (12)
Kennet School, Thatcham

Risks

Risks are what you choose them to be,
Some risks come with a fee.
Risks don't wait for you,
But you wait for risks.
Why do you do what you do?
Because it wouldn't be a risk if you knew.
Questions are risks,
Answers are endless;
That is the risk.
Some risks are negative,
But think of the positive.
Some risks push you forward,
Some hold you back,
But only because of something you lack.
This is a risk
But do I care?
It is also an opportunity,
One that is rare.
Risks are wagers,
Risks are gambles.
Some risks put you in danger,
Some leave you in shambles.
But that one risk, that turns out right,
It will be worth it, for years or one night.
Risks are what you choose them to be.

Pablo Suarez (13)
Kennet School, Thatcham

The Spiral Of Dance

The fizzing instigates,
As the rhythm holds my fate,
Up, down, right and left, this big black void of space;
Nobody around me,
But I still know they're there,
Eyes fixated on me, frozen in mid-air.

The tornado is cascading,
As the world around me is fading,
Enveloped in emotions, everyone's just waiting.

Climbing higher and higher,
Until it reaches the sky,
I can't go on for much longer, the notes continue to fly,
At last the whirlwind's over,
Collapsed on the floor,
The frantic frenzy has been tamed, the dance is no more.

Lucy Moran (13)
Kennet School, Thatcham

Soon We'll Be Gone... But Hold On!

Soon we'll be gone
Every single one.
Our black and white fur,
Will all be a blur.
Poachers do not see,
What they are doing
All they see is the money...

Soon we'll be gone
Every single one.
No place in the zoos
The future will have no clue.
How we were all once
Part of the planet.
Nothing can happen about it, can it?

But guess what?
The WWF has opened to us with a pop.
More of us are being saved,
And we can now be brave.
So we all want to thank WWF,
Because without them,
There would be none of us left.

Kassie Griffiths-Whatley (12)
Kennet School, Thatcham

In The Jungle

Among the canopy of the trees,
Monkeys swing as they please,
And in amongst the leaves,
You can't hear yourself breathe.

Among the canopy of the trees,
Snakes weave as they please,
All the way through the leaves,
Passing the bees.

Among the canopy of the trees,
Birds fly carefully,
Floating through the breeze,
Slowly at ease.

Among the canopy of trees,
Elephants stomp forcefully,
Trumpeting to the trees,
But the king of the jungle will always be,
Me!

Sophie Ford (12)
Kennet School, Thatcham

The Ocean

Waves splashing against the shore,
Rain pattering against the door,
Water moving around in the glass,
Liquids moving around in their mass,
Fish skimming through the waves,
The sea's horizon's just a haze,
Shells washed up on the beach,
The other side of the ocean seems out of reach,
Tidal winds blow through your hair,
To conquer the seas is something no man would ever dare,
To cross the waters is just a notion,
That is the power of the ocean.

Pratik Yadav (13)
Kennet School, Thatcham

Kiwi

National icon of New Zealand,
A land that is mainly green land.
Many predators but not many prey,
The kiwi shy, but says, 'Hey.'
Not safe on the land,
Almost as if it's banned,
Hunting in the costal sand,
Definitely not a dreamland,
Fifty percent of kiwi eggs die,
No guarantee kiwis will survive.
Five percent make it to adulthood,
With harsh forests and wood.
Predators, losing habitats and people,
All killing and being evil.

Abbie Kate Rayns (13)
Kennet School, Thatcham

Shakespeare's Starting

One day Shakespeare was you,
He had troubles to succeed always too.
But he never gave up, stuck to a dream,
Now his work is excellent and supreme.

He wrote poems, stories and tales,
He tried even more after he failed.
Nobody can be him if you can't see,
That mistakes they happen, for you to have victory.

For you to write a poem, it takes time,
Especially if you want; the perfect line.
So if you want to be that wondrous one,
You'd better read these lines and also have fun.

You may shiver as you feel cold,
Wondering what your audience will share, not hold.
But close your eyes, look up high,
Take a deep breath in, now let out a big refreshing sigh.

You may find your homework hard to complete,
He was the same but perseverance is what he liked to repeat.
He tried one day and a tear trickled down,
That was when his talent was found.

His dream had finally come true,
This could now happen to you.

When he sighed just ever so loud,
His brain made that weird sound.

He went to sleep that very day,
He woke up in a phenomenal way.
Thy ideas of a future were laid ahead,
He is still famous, even though he's dead.

Turning into a Shakespeare will take time, for your heart to say its bit,
My revel's ended, it's your turn to say your words, proud while you sit.

Bethany Kenny (12)
Kings Langley School, Kings Langley

Chess

As we begin to play, my hands start to shiver.
The first move is played; a disgusting shiver travels down my spine.
I start to move my trusty pawn.
The second I move it, my brain
Begins to mourn.

Each thought flashing through my head,
Bringing me to my knees, making me cry instead.
The flashing of the lights puts me off my game,
I listen to the distinct mumbling; they are the ones to blame.

Am I open to attack, when can stab the knife in their back?
The strong, eager swipe of a diamond encrusted knife,
The discovered attack revealed, my invincible shield, that
Can shield the taunts, the hurt and doubt.

Am I developing the pieces, when can I start showing my hidden maces,
Weapons that can cut through their defence's flesh and bone, destroying
Their facade which was set like a stone.
With their cunning, they've set multiple traps, I finally see an opening,
I'm navigating this map; finally, they'll close their smug trap.

I've reached the top of the board, I'm calmly, skillfully and
Brilliantly revealing; my hidden sword.
The king's trapped and I start to act with the strong,
eager, swipe of a diamond encrusted knife.

Emmanuel Boakye (14)
Mossbourne Community Academy, Hackney

I Stand Corrected

We were all created for a reason,
And changes need to be made,
Not only by the seasons,
Women sit afraid in a cage,
No hope or freedom,
Fantasising about dreams they have made,
Not able to achieve them,
The genders are immensely uneven.

I stand corrected,
These days in society,
The wrong things are protected,
The wrong things are right,
The salt is sweet,
And the sugar is sour like lime.

I stand corrected,
So take my apology,
Sitting under a shade,
A shade of inequality,
I know women don't obtain the strength of a male,
Proven biologically,
But women fight from their intellectual brains,
Psychologically.

The perpetual, persistent struggles that we face,
Like the poverty, discrimination and the colour of our face,

The struggles are growing and spreading day by day,
This tragic disease that spreads throughout our brains.

So I stand corrected,
You probably think I'm biased,
Since this isn't your perspective,
But I'm just being honest,
From the dreams that have been rejected.

All the women that are affected,
By the hopeless and the liars,
Covering the truth,
Telling you that you can't,
And men are higher.

Their minds are in a state of captivity,
Getting told you can't,
Because it's not a female activity.

But we are all the future of this world,
We are going to achieve great things,
Although we are all girls,
We all have strength,
Because it takes pain to give birth,
Some of the greatest people in history are women,
And have changed this Earth.

They say everyone's equal,
But clearly some are more equal than others,
So if you're women, sisters, daughters and mothers,

Do what you want and achieve your dreams,
Other than the front of the magazine covers.

It's not as hard as it seems,
But gender inequality makes it hard to believe,
In reality, gender is not an issue,
Women are just emotional and sometimes need a tissue,
Sorry for revealing,
But everyone has feelings,
Everyone has emotions because we're all human beings,
But since we are women, we must stay at home, cleaning.

Rosa Parks was a woman,
Struggles filled her heart,
But she thought from her mind,
She fought and denied,
For so long, it's been wrong,
I think it's time to be right.

Living under oppression,
I think it's time to get back what we should have,
But I don't think we would have,
Our human rights,
We would still be living under oppression,
We would still be in cripple chains of segregation,
Humanity's greatest depression.

So I think we should be thankful,
To the women of the past and the present,

Michelle Obama, Rosa Parks and Malala,
Malala made a change,
Because she fought for education,
For girls in our generation,
To nurture young women,
To great achievers of our nation,
There is no limitation,
Everyone can go higher,
Till there is no gravitation.

Every single one of you has a brain worth gold,
To appreciate the sun, you got to know rain,
I know you understand the pain in the world,
So feel free to make a change.

All people dream,
But do not always find,
Those who dream at night,
In the plea of insanity,
In the dusty recesses of their mind,
Wake in the day, to find it was vanity.

All people dream,
But the dreams are not equal,
The dreamers of the day are dangerous people,
For they may act on their dreams, with open eyes,
Life is your dream,
And you're living in your mind.

My intuition goes to war within itself,
As it refuses to judge by someone's gender, race or wealth,
Move forward with your life, instead of stopping someone else,
Stay true to what you believe,
And stay true to yourself.

I stand corrected,
And I will not take a seat,
At the back of the bus, as expected,
I must take a stand,
And I will not take a seat,
I stand corrected.

Zainab Zaidi (13)
Norbury Manor Business & Enterprise College For Girls, Thornton Heath

My Past Ain't My Future

Alright then,
Yes, look, just because I'm here doesn't mean that I'm back,
I ain't here to cause trouble, here to put GU16 on the map,
Yes, sick of your trash, sick of your fake herd,
Sick of the pain, sick of the hurt.

Time to cleanse my soul and show what's right,
Are you ready or not, ready or not?
Couldn't stand last year, made me messed,
Caused every bit of hate I had
You said I was unstable, said I was a mess,
Thought you could tell me what to do; but now I'm here, like what you gonna
do?
I wish I could turn back the time, when people didn't know me,
When people hadn't heard of me, when people didn't judge me,
Would take back everything, apart from family.

Hated the fact that I'm the factor,
Hated it that I was a chapter; yeah.
Now you wanna click up after all your mistakes; ha,
I looked in your face; you're not the same?

But they don't know me, but they know my team,
#louisjames; yeah that's me,
If you get caught snitching, get a slash on your cheek,
Or worse than that, yes...

Got one with my mum and left to the street,
Ran to my mates, knocked on the door,
He was like, 'Who are you with? Why and what for?'
I was like, 'Here, call the feds, can't stand this; my life is a mess.'
5 minutes later at the door, 'Can I talk to Louis?' 'Yeah what for?'
I was like, 'Here, it was a big incident,'
Mum said, 'This was a coincidence.'
I was like, 'Stop hitting me, it's just not fair,'
She was like, 'Yeah, well, it's fair; yeah it's fair.'
Now it's been one year, one call it's back, one shout, one slap; that's fact.
Told her I couldn't do this any more, so instead of fighting I ran out the door,
What am I doing now? Making raps, not bothered about pay
'Cause what happened in the past, is what made me who I am today.

Louis Gaunt (12)
North West Surrey Short Stay School - Kingsway Centre, Woking

My Sister

Her birth was the most beautiful thing that ever occurred to me,
There she was, in front of me,
She was asleep as I sat beside her,
Then I saw something, no one would believe,
Because right there and right then; I could swear I saw a faint smile.
I still have that memory stuck in my head,
As if it were superglued to my mind.
Day by day, month by month, she grew,
She grew up into an amazing girl,
Beautiful, smart and all the qualities I ever wished for.
She was the one who brought light to my life,
She was always there when I needed her the most,
And in return I would do the same.
I love going through the journey of life together,
And I wish it would last forever.

Hadi Hussain Kizhakkevattooli (12)
Orleans Park School, Twickenham

Last Night

I was laying flat inside
Hands outstretched, head up supine

When I suddenly fell upon my buttocks
My body flipped me out
For it entered, the holy land of slumber
It wanted me to show it places
Places too far to go, places too surreal, too slow

I started walking on the dew kissed grass
The petrichor had me wild
It made me crave home
The hiraeth was setting on me like mist over sea

Tonight, I wanted to go home
Tonight, I'd take my body to the iridescent streets of my childhood
To the streets with ill-parked cars
And tiny, flowery parks

I held my somnambulant self by its fingers
And travelled thousands of miles
In a fraction of time
Only to be welcomed by the aroma of my mother's curries
And my friends' voice, which now had turned slurry

This place is so tiny, so low
But there's something about it, which wouldn't get me bored

I was about to hug my mum when I see bright phosphenes in the room
It was me, rubbing my eyes
Sigh, it was time to go
Back to my room, shimmering in broad daylight
Back to the world, where everything is so nice.

Somriddho Dasgupta (16)
Padworth College, Reading

Until You Take A Look

Think of me as a fortune cookie,
You'll never know what's inside of me;
Until you take a look.

Some people have a wonder,
A minute or two to ponder.
But they'll never know what's inside of me;
Until they take a look.

They think they know my brain,
Or if I'm feeling pain.
But they'll never know what's inside of me;
Until they take a look.

That's like guessing the end of a story,
Before you read the book.
You'll never know what's inside of it;
Until you take a look.

So next time you see a ginger,
A blonde or a brunette,
Think, *I'll never know what they're like,*
Until I introduce myself.

Kate Ford (12)
Prendergast-Hilly Fields College, Brockley

The Lies We Tell

Stop. Watch. Observe.
Turn around and swerve your head to see,
People walking in the streets,
Women and men,
Bodies attached to heads.
Society's proudest creation, working, living,
Experiencing the given.
But wait, it's fake and now it's too late,
Mobiles, briefcases, a multi-culture of these faces are lying.
Look, the man on your left; is trying his best, to hide from his wife that he was underneath another woman's dress,
And the woman beside you, doesn't know what to do, because her boss is too violent and touches her too.
And it is not okay. None of it is okay. But we do it anyway.
No matter how many times you wash them,
Your hands are still dirty from what lays upon them,
And the things you have done with them -
Are unerasable.

We swallow things whole because we don't want our loved ones to know what happened at work that day.
The woman beside you has a husband she lies to because she is scared and needs the pay.
The husband is sick and hasn't worked for six months and she is the only thing keeping the family afloat.

The bruises on her arms, the scars, the memories turned
dark are punishments for her, but for him,
The man on your left,
They are trophies.

Quick, slick, don't miss a trick,
He sees her walking in, into work that day,
Jumps onto her like prey, but she doesn't complain,
She needs the pay.
He doesn't care about fair or whether she gives consent,
He just carries on pulling her hair,
There, and again tomorrow.
Quick, zipper-up, tie straightened,
He changes the lock on the door to vacant.
He wipes the corner of his mouth before shoving her out the
door,
Hard enough for her to fall to the floor but he doesn't care,
He's done for the day and she knows she will get her pay -
Maybe.

At the end of the day, they both go their separate ways,
He to your left and she right beside you.
She pulls down her sleeves so nobody sees,
The marks on her arm from where he gripped her a little too
hard and he,
The man on your left,

He goes back to his wife, his kids,
The nice home he has, where nobody knows but him,
Just what happened at work that day.
Crack, *snap*, opens up a beer can,
He rests his feet on the cushioned stool while his daughter sits on his lap telling him about school.
As his evening draws to a close and he removes his clothes then changes into night wear.
His wife is on the bed, humming a tune that is stuck in her head and she is reading a book before tucking into bed, the girl with the dragon tattoo,
Clueless of who is lying next to her.

While, the woman beside you goes back to her husband,
Doesn't want to touch him,
Doesn't want to infect him with what happened at work that day.
They sit down and share a meal; potatoes and veal,
Table cloth of teal and a documentary about seals playing on the TV.
He watches the TV and she watches him watch the TV and she hopes, begs that he knows, suspects.
He doesn't.

And you?
Well now you are sandwiched.
You're stuck between two strangers' lies,
Unable to unpluck the strings that tie them together.

But wait, why should you try?
These people are strangers to your eyes and as long as it is not you that cries, why do you care?
So off you go, back to your day,
Tomorrow you'll forget all about yesterday.

Maya Nagra (14)
Prendergast-Hilly Fields College, Brockley

There Is A Word Named Like...

There is a word named 'like'.
'Like' a bee
'Like' the sea
Just, 'like' me

It's been programmed to enter
my world of words,
Crashing into my sentences,
Like a descending firebird.

Leaving chaos in its wake,
Out of control,
An earthquake,
Fire on my lips,
As my words flow and roll.

It somehow travels to my mouth
and slips
from my lips
like a tiny fleeing mouse from its hole.

'Like',
I'm going to the shops and,
'Like',
I was wondering if you wanted to,
'Like',
Come with me?

I don't understand - how did it escape?
I have no input in this thing
How and why has it got no zing?

My mother highlights this word in blue
screams and shouts around the house,
'You're like a scratched record',
It really makes me bored!

Stop with the 'like', and find a new word!

I just repeat and repeat
and repeat
the word which I wish
I could simply just eat.

I must find a new and shiny word
Something that will impress the clever and superb
One day 'like' will never again be heard
Something forgotten, a shadow of a word.

One day I will conquer the 'like',
The word I sleep with throughout the night
It will one day disappear and I'll be left,
Free and clear.

So here is a list of my favourite words
Plinth, grimace, flinch and turd
Sparkle, twinkle, gangly and absurd
Wink, slop...

But oh yes...

My favourite word has to be...
Plop.

Ruby Rebecca Stanhope (11)
Prendergast-Hilly Fields College, Brockley

A Door In A Wall

Let's say there is a wall,
Nothing special, just a wall,

And in that wall there is a door,
Not locked, or open, just a door,

And on the other side, there is...
Well, nobody knows.

And nobody will open the door,
Because nobody wants to,
And nobody can,

And if nobody wants to,
And nobody can,

No one will know what's on the other side.

But if somebody did open the door;
Someone who's a little too curious,
And a little too brave,

And if that someone who's a little too curious,
And a little too brave,

Opens the door...

Well, would that be right?

Eleanor Houusden (13)
Prendergast-Hilly Fields College, Brockley

The Books I Love

The books I love, fit snug in my hand,
The pages turn by unconscious command.
Essential are the pages, that flap and fold,
Not those pages that stay white and look cold.
I must be able to feel a book's length,
And not measure my progress by percent.

I don't quite know the book of my dreams,
Would it be small or would it go to extremes?

They must have bright covers and not dull plastic,
But about a thin card, I can be most enthusiastic.
The glow from the page must not be artificial,
Otherwise the effect can be quite superficial.
And to books that require Wi-Fi, I often don't comply,
But sometimes needs must and I reluctantly adjust.

I don't quite know the book of my dreams,
Would it be small or would it go to extremes?

They pile up on shelves and cover the floors,
Some can be found in attics, and others behind doors.
Books turn yellow and gather dust,
But guard and protect them all, I must.
There should be a place for every book to stay,
Because each book has a moment, a day.

I don't quite know the book of my dreams,
Would it be small or would it go to extremes?

The Kindle is king, the iPad is queen,
Soon there won't be a book to be seen.
Not before long books will disappear,
And that, my friends, is my greatest fear.
So give your books, those on the shelves,
A second look, before they're quelled.

Isabelle Mary Crawford (11)
Prendergast-Hilly Fields College, Brockley

GCSE Pressures

They say who can't hear-
will surely feel,
But yet I haven't felt it,
I find it hard to balance my education -
with just being a teenager,
I set a foundation,
I need to climb up the ladder,

There's an envelope foreshadowing my future,
Missing the feeling of nature,
An envelope of opportunity,
But yet my immaturity -
hasn't changed,
Too blessed to be stressed,

They say the grass is greener -
on the other side,
But yet I couldn't be any cleaner,
I still cried,
And dried my tears,
I still tried,
Beating my fears,

I spend my days gazing upon pages,
Revision takes ages,

Pages filled with information,
I don't know how to function,
Knowing this will all be over soon,
Too blessed to be stressed,

They say my life -
is about to change,
But it's fine to be stressed,
Mama never raised a stereotype,
I am a person of significance,
I have the skill of remembrance,

Confidence battle,
Having to paddle,
Don't need money to be happy,
Don't want to be changing a nappy,
I want to be proud,
Too blessed to be stressed,

They say you have a voice -
so use it,
But my opinion is irrelevant,
I find it hard to believe,
That someone, somewhere -
would love to be in my position,

As I continue my love-hate relationship, with my education.
Too blessed to be stressed.

Monique Kathleen Stewart (15)
Prendergast-Hilly Fields College, Brockley

Tangy Chicken

Finger-licking chicken,
By the New Cross line,
Tangy spice is thrilling,
By the phone shop shrine.

Fingers holding bones,
That were cut with a chop.
By the mighty lady,
Of jerk chicken shop.

Blackened air surrounds me,
As the setting sun bleeds red.
Take that air and wrap it up,
Hold it till you're dead.

Cause it's that finger-licking chicken,
By the New Cross line.
Tangy spice is thrilling,
And it's just on time.

Fingers holding bones,
As the teeth rip and tear.
In the...
Crunchy, tangy, juicy, thrilling,
New Cross air.

Edith Anne Baggott (12)
Prendergast-Hilly Fields College, Brockley

Me And You

When I look in the mirror I see me
When I look in at you, I see me... but older.

My journey has just begun,
When yours has had many miles.

My heart is young and beating fast,
Your heart is old and slowing down.

I'm just gaining my experience,
Whilst you are as wise as an owl.

I have breathed many breaths,
Just not as many as you.

The world is exciting and new,
When you have seen it through,

But we still enjoy the happiness and laughter
surrounding us...

Because we are still one,
No matter how old.

Neve Hathaway (12)
Prendergast-Hilly Fields College, Brockley

A Horse

A horse,
That lurks around my brain,
Which causes me to complain,
The way they can be so vain;
Drives me insane.

And as soon as my mind is clear,
They rapidly reappear,
Galloping into my mind; they leave the stable behind.

People expect them to go, like a thunderbolt
But they suddenly come to a halt,
However, it's not their fault.

I love them ever so much,
But many people are scared to touch,
It is impossible to forget their beautiful mane;
Which slips between my rein.

Sorcha O'Leary (11)
Prendergast-Hilly Fields College, Brockley

Five Views Of Trump

A little boy, only eleven,
Should quite frankly be living in Heaven,
If he's the son of the billionaire Trump,
But right now, he's down in the dumps.
I know it's wrong, he has more money,
Than at least one hundred kids.
But did he deserve this?
Cyberbullied because of his dad,
This made him really sad.

Lots of women feeling down
Because an old man is being a clown
Drilling thoughts in their heads,
'Women are objects,' he said.
Even celebrities won't play along,
Because they feel it all went wrong.
Lots of opportunities to take,
But they will refuse them straight.

Now what is the president getting out of this?
More money, more power, this is it.
He doesn't care for the health and happiness of others,
He doesn't have time for fathers and mothers,
If racism calls knocking at his door,
Peace and harmony are no more.

Sophie Cosham (12)
Ratton School, Eastbourne

Rainbow At Heart

As a child,
You're always told to stay true to yourself,

Your parents would sit you down in the living room, and they'd lecture you about: 'Always believe in yourself!' or 'Never change yourself for anyone!'

You'd let them talk, not taking much notice, letting it go in one ear and out the other.
After, you'd go back to your mates, and talk about sport or who had a crush on who, or how your evil teacher gave you extra homework.

You kept your secret untold,
A secret kept close to your heart.
You went into school the next day,
Now let the story unfold...

'Weirdo! Gay!'

You'll hear the bullies slur, while they kick and punch and beat you to the ground,
Over and over again.
For the one person you told, snitched on you to the whole school,
And now you're here, at the back of the class, feeling lonely and sad,
'Cause you gave in and believed what they said.

At the end of the lesson, your teacher asked you to stay behind,
The rest of the class shouting, 'Oooohhhh!'
Your teacher asks what's wrong with you,
And all the words tumble out.
'They call me names!'
'They kick and beat me at school!'
'They follow me home!'
'They taunt me, they make me feel horrible!'

She told me it's okay, and that I should be proud of who I was,
To be proud of who I was,
If only I listened to what my parents said. Rainbow at heart.

Kurdi Ahmad (12)

Ratton School, Eastbourne

The Pain Of Power

The pain of power is one who possesses all,
The pain of power is what makes great men fall.
The pain of power, as silent as the night,
For it drives men into the depths of regret, no forgiveness in sight.

No matter how wilful you may be,
You will fall, like many before me.
Its devil-like face carved in a log,
Or that mysterious face you see in the fog.

This confusing picture appearing in mind,
Will leave all strength and intelligence behind.
Devote yourself to avoiding this disaster,
And as they fall - the importance of your life will go much faster.

Yours sincerely,
Secret of the night.

Joe Whitmore (11)
Ratton School, Eastbourne

Sport

I lace up the trainers, pull on the shirt,
Run on the pitch, get caked in dirt.

Score the goal, win the game,
Hold up the trophy, put the other team to shame.

Go to bed, dream of that goal,
Let that winning streak unroll.

As I run away from all the bad things,
I wonder what tomorrow brings.

Will I win the game, score the goal?
Well it doesn't matter really.

Just take part,
That's a start.

Don't worry about winning,
It's the taking part that counts...

Jasmine Price (11)
Ratton School, Eastbourne

Brexit

Who's idea was this?
This was no one's wish.
Why must we leave?
We will not succeed.
Many wanted to stay,
But to their dismay.

Theresa May said, 'No way,'
For many it was a terrible day,
David Cameron on that day would not have it,
So he stopped and let them have it.
Brexit was its name,
It was a political game.

What can we do,
We're finished through and through,
We have nothing to lose,
It's yesterday's news.

Gorazd Stojanovski (12) & George
Ratton School, Eastbourne

Homework

Why should there be homework?
All it does to you is strangle your brain in times when you don't need it to,
We do enough at school.
Teachers say we should do our homework, when? Why?
Just why?

The weekends are meant to be free,
I cannot spend time with my family; as I am doing homework.
My friends, well whilst they're out and about having fun, I'm stuck in my room, staring at the wall, doing homework,
Why?
Just why?

Michael Morehen (11)
Ratton School, Eastbourne

When The Experts Hate

They think they know best,
But truly they don't
They say what they say
But all they mean is *hate*
I mean should they ban people,
For doing nothing wrong?
Should people run from horrid places,
To have *hate* thrown in their faces?
We believe the answer is no.
But what if *hate* began to spread
And blame was placed on innocent people?
This is what happens,
When the experts *hate*.

Lily Vater (12) & Ernest Connolly (12)
Ratton School, Eastbourne

Difference

Have different colour hair
Have different colour skin
Speak a different language
Have a belief
A boy doing something girls do
A girl wearing boys clothes
It doesn't matter
We're glad that everyone is here with us
Just remember it's okay to be different
Everyone can be different
Everyone can be different!

Oliver Hover (11)
Ratton School, Eastbourne

Sara Bukai

No one leaves home,
unless home is the jaws of a lion.
You only flee to the border and beyond,
when everyone else is fleeing as well.

On my left,
my local shopkeeper,
panting...
fear turning him wild.

On my right,
my once timid neighbour,
charging through his friends to get closer,
closer to the peace.

The boy who was in my maths class,
who always made us laugh,
is holding a gun bigger than his body.
You only flee when,
there is nothing left to stay for.

The world needs to know,
that people wouldn't place their loved ones in a boat,
unless land is more dangerous than water.

No one climbs into the belly,
of a lorry or truck,
unless those many miles travelled,
are more than just a journey.

No one scales walls,
or scrambles under barbed wire fences,
unless that chance of not being caught,
is valued above their life,
and lives of their family.

No one fakes a passport or lies to the police,
unless they know, they are safer in prison...
than at home.

No one chooses refugee camps,
unless they have more chance of living there,
than a city in flames.

Could you take it?
No one is made of titanium,
no one's skin is tough enough...

Dirty immigrants, asylum seekers,
the money takers, the job stealers,
terrorists, criminals.

How can we swallow these comments?
Maybe it's because this abuse,
is softer than watching everyone you love,
snatched from your life.
Bullets and bombs,
creating more and more orphans.

No one leaves home,
unless your pride has to be forgotten,
and the world around you,
is ripped and torn to pieces.
Sticks and stones may break my bones,
and Western worlds still hurt me.

Isabel Harber (13)
St Albans Girls' School, St Albans

She'll Be Gone Soon

Those big, sad eyes
That always look past me
That fluffy tail;
That constantly gets clumpy

She'll be gone soon.

The house will be so empty,
Without her pottering around.
There'll be no furry ball;
That doesn't resemble a hound.

She'll be gone soon.

The bad days are starting to
Outnumber the good.
Some days she's leaping for joy,
Just like in her puppyhood.

She'll be gone soon.

Most days, she just lies there.
It's hard to tell if she's actually breathing,
A pile of bones
Though sometimes she starts wheezing.

She'll be gone soon.

She eats what she needs;
To keep going day to day.
She rarely has enough energy,
To even stand up and walk away.

She'll be gone soon.

It could be this week or the next,
But all we know;
Is that we really don't want
Those big, sad eyes to go.

Isabelle Kinghorn (15)
St Albans Girls' School, St Albans

Glory Days

Some say that animals have no emotions,
That they don't feel or think like we do.
Others say that animals are all savage beasts,
That they are the monsters of this world
But the true monsters,
The real monsters,
Are us.
Mankind is the monster, that destroys and kills.
They are the destroyer,
The devourer.
They are the snake, who slowly eats its own tail -
The one who murders their own flesh and blood.
What happened to those glory days?
Take a look at what you've done!
Are you happy with your tyrant's heart?
Unless you stop your foolish ways,
Nothing is ever going to change,
Think of your children, your brothers, your sisters
Think of your parents, husbands and wives
Would you like it if they were taken;
To be a trophy or even an item?
A piece of clothing to be worn?
There once was a time, when birds ruled the skies,
And the seals would swim happily,
As elephants travelled the land

If you don't stop now my friends;
We will never again see the glory days.

Namam Kadir (13)
St Albans Girls' School, St Albans

Untitled

These un-motivational voices rushing through my head.
So many choices!
The pressure of doing well, the embarrassment of failing,
why do we have such awful things.
Let your wings free!
They say well, how can we?
When you're clinging onto our every word.
We are not just little birds, in a blurred world.
'Don't give up', is what they say, well then there should be
no such thing as right or wrong!
God chooses when and where we need to fight the world,
it's not up to anyone else.
That's what makes us give up.
If you don't succeed at first, then oh well, one test shouldn't
be able to ruin your whole life.
We don't need to prove to anyone, that we are the best.
What you personally do with it and achieve with it, should
be your own decision, not the pressure of parents or
grandparents.
Believe in yourself!
Not all of us need to be a businessperson, snob.
Don't listen to what they say, be your own person, it doesn't
matter if you're wealthy or not, you don't need a well-paid
job,
To be a somebody, you are you, and no one else!

Anahitaa Hariyani (12)
St Clement Danes School, Chorleywood

I Am Twelve

I am twelve
I don't have answers
I don't even know the question
But I know a lot of people
Who talk, as if they do.

Mum and dad say
'Study hard
So you end up with some options
Get a job
Make some money
Have a family of your own.
Love your brothers and sister
Take your shoes off
Don't slam doors
Eat your breakfast
Do your homework
Don't wear make-up.'
Is that all?

Friends say
'Got no boyfriend? - Loser!
You will end up on your own.
Perfect pretty, perfect body
Perfect's all you need to be'

Whilst at the same time,
'Don't go changing
Don't you change yourself one bit.
True is what you've got to be
True to yourself and to me.'

And celebrities say it too,
'Don't go changing
Don't do drugs
Don't smoke anything
Do buy our stuff
Do like us on Facebook.
Give your time and
Give your money
To the charities we rate.'
(Do as I say, not as I do)
Well, come on -
They live that way?

So I end up on the iPad
And I type a single question
To the god of knowledge - Google,
'What's the meaning of this life?'
24/7 quotes it offers,
And the top of them's Camus.

He seems to say it all quite nicely
So I'll pass it on to you:

You will never be happy if you continue to search for what happiness consists of.
You will never live if you are looking for the meaning of life.

Estella Woodhead (12)
St Clement Danes School, Chorleywood

The Age Of Racism

What age does a racist become a racist?
When does a classroom joke become a racist slur?
In primary school, racist opinions were not frequently shared,
They remained private, fearful of the teacher's glare.

On starting at secondary, children try to 'be cool',
To gain others' attention, they act like a fool.
One person's sarcasm can be interpreted as harm,
The speaker thinks it's funny, the victim sees no charm.

Skin colours and religions can be abused in jest,
But to a sensitive soul, they will feel highly stressed.
Should the victim fight back or walk away in peace?
Report it to the teacher, or even the police?

Retaliation can be harmful; it doesn't need to be so,
Better to report the crime to someone in the know.
For a crime it is, that will be punished...
Suspension? Expulsion? Don't be astonished!

If you think you're a racist, control your tongue,
Much better that everyone tries to get along.

Charlotte Barnett (12)
St Clement Danes School, Chorleywood

Christmas

Frosty days and ice-still nights,
Christmas trees, filled up with lights,
Sound of reindeer in the snow,
That was Christmas long ago.

Mistletoes are in place,
Giggles around the small fireplace,
Gifts wrapped under the Christmas tree bow,
That is Christmas now.

Children open presents with shouts of glee,
While lots of teenagers go out to ski,
Christmas lights and candles glow,
That was Christmas long ago.

Winter skates and fun sleigh rides,
Children love their mums' sweet delights,
Snowflakes rest on the window panes and glow,
That is Christmas now.

Christmas pudding is being shared,
Sweet-voiced carols, fill the fresh air,
Stockings hanging in rows,
That was Christmas long ago.

The radio and the TV is on,
Christmas with the family, dad and mum,
Christmas lights are all over the town,
That is Christmas now.

Starry nights, so beautiful and blue,
Friends are calling out to you,
Christmas would never make you slow,
That was Christmas long ago.

Christmas has changed over the years,
Many people celebrate Christmas here,
Every year, Christmas beams,
And gives everyone amazing dreams.

Magarishi Chandra (11)
St Clement Danes School, Chorleywood

I'm Coming

You're there when I wake up
You're there on my phone
You're there in the hallway
You're there in my home.

Rumours, gossiping, teasing and threats
I'm not sure who to turn to next
Harassment, dares, whispering and lies
With only my pillow to hear my cries.

When I'm online
I know you're there
You screenshot my pictures
It's really not fair.

When you're spiteful and mean
I pretend not to mind
I just can't get rid of you
You're really unkind.

People will watch and do nothing at all
I really just need to leave this school
This bully will never leave me alone
You just sit, watch upon your throne.

You're under my skin and under my bed
I just want to get you out of my head
So I need to stand up, I need to be strong
To prove to myself, that you're in the wrong.

You think that you're strong and I am weak
Bully, I'm coming for you, with a punch in the cheek.

Lexie Cinelli (11)
St Clement Danes School, Chorleywood

The Making Of A War

Countries,
Neighbours,
Friends,
Only a border separating them.
A murmur of disagreement,
The posting of an angry opinion on social media,
A swarm of replies:
Provocative,
Insulting,
Mocking,
Scattered agreements in-between.
Crowds gathered to protest,
Furious talks between their two leaders,
A sense of panic in the air.
War is declared!
Who shall win the right to own the border?
Armies gather,
A long snake of war vehicles, all travelling to battle,
Thousands of troops in trucks,
Thundering tanks,
Planes roaring through the air.
Waves of civilians flee,
Not knowing, if they'll ever see, their loved ones again.

Bullets fired,
Soldiers dying,
Destruction everywhere,
Buildings reduced to rubble,
Still the raging war goes on...

Luca Matharu (12)
St Clement Danes School, Chorleywood

Bully

You pull me, push me,
Never say sorry...
All you do is make me worry.
Your sexist, racist, homophobic comments,
Is it okay to be different?
The words you call out, hurt me the most,
Even if it is only a joke or even if you start to boast.
What did I ever do to you?
You steal, you shout, you make up lies,
When I get home, I sit in my room and cry.
In my head, I just want to die.

I want to move schools,
But that's not an answer.
I am going to stand tall,
Speak out and not fall.
It's time I do something,
And not leave it at nothing.
Face my anxieties, that you make me feel,
I am robust and as strong as steel.
You are a bully, just go away and stop.

Frankie Owen (12)
St Clement Danes School, Chorleywood

Hope

Sleeping in a doorway with my only friend, my dog,
It's freezing cold, I'm lonely, my mind is just a fog.
I really don't like this life, it really gets me down,
People never smile at me, they always tut and frown.

I had a dream the other night, that woke me with a start,
It was all about my life before it was torn apart.
I had a house, a family and a job with real good pay,
Now all that's gone and I'm just here, in this doorway.

But every day I really try to make things much better,
I have applied for a new job, I am waiting for a letter.
But until that time, Johnny and I will cope,
I know it will all be right, all I can do is hope.

Millie Beetham (11)
St Clement Danes School, Chorleywood

A Poem For The Homeless

The world needs to change for the better
No more fancy jumpers and sweaters
We can just walk out and jump on a bus
When there are people out there who need us
There are families on the streets, who long for money
You walk past them every day and think it's funny
But if the freezing pavement was your bed
Wouldn't you be crying instead?
In the cold winter months, we have a warm fire
But they are at the end of their wire
Just help these poor people, they had great lives once
Give them your presence
Talk to them, buy them some food and just be nice
You don't have to do it twice
But that doesn't matter
It's what you do that matters.

Sam Carroll (12)
St Clement Danes School, Chorleywood

The Poachers

All the poachers walk up the muddy footpath
Leading down to the wild animals
With their guns at the ready the only noise that could be heard
Is the roaring of the lions and the howling of the monkeys

The expanse comes into view
The predators are ready to pounce
The poachers are ready to shoot
As the sun goes behind the clouds
The atmosphere becomes intense

The shot is heard
The animal shudders
And falls on the dry dusty dirt track

The stampede has started
The other animals flee into the distance
Silence falls over the landscape

The smell of death is in the air
The poachers have won.

Jake Giggs-Jones (12)
St Clement Danes School, Chorleywood

The Way We See Each Other

Hurting people all around
Like a plague throughout a town
Thoughts, actions, movements and feelings
We are all the same, we are human beings
People are treated unequally
Because of race, appearance or disability
Think about the way we want to be treated
With compliments, smiles, be nicely greeted
Fights, arguments, bullies and gangs
Give nasty thoughts to bring you down
But let's all change the way we see each other
It doesn't matter about size and colour
We all should stop, with the pointless hate
And should be there, for one another
Let's change for the future
And then again
Feel like we all belong again.

Lucy Millard (12)
St Clement Danes School, Chorleywood

Suspense

The time is here
My heart is pumping fast
People pacing up and down
Cold floorboards, creaking underfoot.

A sea of white suits floating
Moving quickly from left to right, up and down,
Punching the air, with snapping movements
Tense feelings all around.

My name is called out...
I run to the front of the line
Adrenaline rushing through my veins
Sweat dripping down my collar
As I focus on my goal...

I finish...

I sit nervously back down, onto a hard, wooden, knobbly gym bench
Waiting for my name to be called again
Have I passed,
Have I failed...

James Todd (12)
St Clement Danes School, Chorleywood

War Never Changes

Cities are bombed
People become scared
Economies fall
Because war never changes.

People are killed
Fear spreads quickly
Families are split
Because war never changes.

Supplies become scarce
Rationing begins
People starve
Because war never changes.

New alliances form
Old alliances fall
Dictators reign
Because war never changes.

Innocents die
Futures are destroyed
Everyone suffers
Because war never changes.

Daniel Joseph Amedume (12)
St Clement Danes School, Chorleywood

What Is Wrong With The World?

We are all different shapes and sizes,
We all have different likes and dislikes,
But nothing changes who we are.
What is wrong with the world is
How we treat each other.
Just because we have enemies
Doesn't mean we can't be friends.
We judge each other by the people we
Think they are, but we never stop and
Realise what their story is behind them.
Before you judge someone by their cover,
Have a read inside.
You might realise they are not
So different from you.

Megan Louise Butler (11)
St Clement Danes School, Chorleywood

Syria

Bang, there goes another bomb.
And I realise, nothing can be done.
All the tear gas, makes me sick,
But it's nothing compared to what's in the skip.

The gunfire is terrifying,
The bombs are loud,
The attackers are frightening,
Suddenly, there's a crowd.
My family has been taken,
So has the house,
I'm lying there shaken,
Like a church mouse.

Syria, I love you so,
But I've realised, that it's time to go.

Luke Perera (11)
St Clement Danes School, Chorleywood

Pollution

Dust, dust, engulfs the air,
Pollution is everywhere.
Towns, cities, and villages are dark and gloomy,
Covered under a thick duvet of mankind's waste.
Men, women and children are getting ill.
A great cloud of disease and destruction lingers,
Making people cough and splutter.
You can only smell the foul smoke,
You can only hear the murmuring engines,
You can only taste the decay.
Because dust, dust engulfs the air,
Pollution is everywhere.

Simran-Lily Mudhar (11)
St Clement Danes School, Chorleywood

Bullying/Hate

Is not cool, it makes you look like a fool.
You think you're big, but you're actually small;
It's coming to too much hate, people don't love their mother, nor one another.
There is going to be war, but I just want no more.
People die, cry, lie, just why?
People hate for a living, but we all know it's the beginning.
Don't judge too quick, let's make these ends and let's become friends.

Omer Ogredici (11)
St Clement Danes School, Chorleywood

Make A Difference

Poverty.
Inequality.
People treated differently;
The hungry,
The thirsty,
The poor,
The dirty.

And of course, to us it doesn't matter,

But let's make that difference;
All over the world, in different extremes,
People need to cling to their dreams.
They need the chance to live better lives,
But if nothing is said,

They will be dead.

Pollyanna Dickinson (11)
St Clement Danes School, Chorleywood

Innocence

Children bound to the ground,
Finding their way, through the lost and found,
Faces full of fear,
Fighting like donkeys and deer,

Cornered in their rooms,
Sweeping up with brooms,
Trying to shout for help,
Bellow, shout, yelp,

Abused by their parents,
Running to their grandparents,
Crying their eyes out,
What were they fighting about?

Maya Chudasama (12)
St Clement Danes School, Chorleywood

War

War is revenge,
War is hate,
Darkness lies upon us,
Peace must wait.

Hope is history,
Pain is here,
Bombs rain down,
You're cloaked in fear.

You put up a fight but you lose,
And that leads to tears.
Tears lead to despair.
Despair leads to anger.
Anger leads to hate and hate leads to... more hate.
Hate only ever breeds.

Dexter Simpkins (11)
St Clement Danes School, Chorleywood

Homelessness

I am freezing cold, lying on the streets
I have nothing but thin sheets between me and the cold hard ground
No one cares about me, starving on the side of the road
Looks of fear, if they come too near
My once smart uniform, is now soiled and torn
A life serving my country is ignored
Cowering in the rain, trying to block out the pain
Do not think you could not be the same.

Charlotte Bard (12)
St Clement Danes School, Chorleywood

A Brighter Tomorrow

Today there's another tragedy in the news
Foolish behaviour from people, who have nothing to lose
They never think about the consequences or pain
But are focused on not taking the blame.

Learn from the past and spread laughter and love
Believe in the good and rise above
The world can be a great place
Don't return it with disgrace.

Ella Mae Bishop (12)
St Clement Danes School, Chorleywood

Human

We're all humans, alike, you and me
So why do we treat each other differently?
So stop turning away the refugees,
Because there are loads more than just two or three.
You let them cry, with no sympathy
And you let them die, with no dignity.

Ethan Botwright (12)
St Clement Danes School, Chorleywood

The Other Way Round

I wonder if the Devil is meant to be evil
I wonder why authors write books
about monsters,
They're told to hate and go against humankind,
But is that the true story of their feelings inside?

I wonder if they share better than us?
I wonder if they love and care for all
but I find that's not the story at all
People do not know,
but seem to decide
that the so-called 'devils' don't have a heart inside

I wonder if they have a family?
I wonder if they care
more than us, that they might look after their
world and share with us
If we just let 'them know' that all the stories
we have let them go
then maybe, maybe they will be the heroes,
saving the day keeping the real 'darkness away!'

I wonder, I wonder what they must think
Since they might not be evil
I just have to think
that all this telling and all these stories
are not fair and show no glory,
as we do not know the truth inside

so we need to put these meanings aside
and find the truth of who the 'devils' are, in our minds
to discover the thoughts that are hidden inside

Maybe I'm wrong
but I've got a feeling
that stories are stories
and believing is believing,
could it be?
Maybe...
The other way round.

Bethany Smith
St Mary's Catholic School, Windhill

Death Because Of Gangs

Death is like the devil in disguise.
Dark and dingy, it gives you a surprise.
The next thing you know, you'll be up in the skies,
Popped in the head by God's security guys.
All you can hear is your wife's surprised cries.
You were jumped by gang members,
Then you just remembered,
Bang, bang, they popped you in the dome,
Bang, bang, they took your phone.
Bang, bang, you were left alone,
Then your wife was on the phone.
The cops came and took you away,
Your wife will not forget that day.
She is crying away.

Casey William Wheeler (12)
The Drive Prep School, Hove

Abuse

A s the parents whisper in her ear,
B eginning to hear, I say, 'Oh dear, oh dear.'
U nder the bed, I try to go under
S uddenly, parents, stamping with thunder.
E very day I run away.

Leaving with shame and really bad pain
Leaving with shame and really bad pain
Leaving with shame and really bad pain
I know now that I will never feel the same.

Issy Al-Shimmeri (11)
The Drive Prep School, Hove

Forest

As I saw the collapsing trees
I stopped, stood still and wondered.
Why do people cut down trees?
And what about the poor old bear?
Animals blundering there,
Walking into steaming-hot fire, that scalds and burns.
So colourful, bright and shining
Just like the light of the pale moon glistening and
Shining on the lifeless space of the land,
That was once a forest.

Ethan Goodchild (12)
The Drive Prep School, Hove

Torn Apart

As I run, I feel like I'm in a trance.
I hope I can get there, while there's a chance.
Crack! Bang! The machine with raging yellow claws
Tears up the land and chews it in its jaws.
I see it's no use.
Everything I ever had, I was going to lose.
As the monster slowly tears my world apart,
My feelings overwhelm my mind and my heart...

Corinna Kampalis (11)
The Drive Prep School, Hove

Wouldn't It...

Wouldn't it be lovely,
If there was a storm one day,
That washed all the bad things away.

Wouldn't it be lovely,
If there was a breeze every day,
That woke us up;
And cleaned us up.

Wouldn't it be lovely,
If there was no war and hate in this world.
Wouldn't it be lovely?

Zara Mrkonja (12)
The Drive Prep School, Hove

My Cat. My Games

The thing I love most about my day,
Is coming home to play
With my cat.
It makes my day.
I love my cat.
She is so fat.
I love my cat.

The thing I love most about my day,
Is coming home to play
With my video games.
It makes my day.
I love my games.
I love my games.

Julian Gjona (11)
The Drive Prep School, Hove

Animal Rights

Animals need their rights.
People drain them of fight.
You can see the pain in their sight,
Towering above with such height.
They want to take flight,
Their hearts full of fright.
Always feel like it's night.
Someone needs to show them the light.

Tara Robilliard (11)
The Drive Prep School, Hove

Fishing For My Life

Everything's a blur.
The last thing I remember was my friends in fiery flames,
They were all screaming in agonising pain,
And I did nothing to stop it.

I saw the General's guts on the floor,
His eyes wide open,
It was as if he had this supernatural power,
Of looking into my soul.

Bang!
Went the bombs, *bang!*
Bang!
They were as loud as the sirens in my head,
Alerting me to run,
But I am as stiff as a brick,
My hands numb,
My body quivering,
It was as if I was no longer on Earth,
But in a demonic world!

Zombies lurk in the distance,
I gaze at the spectres,
They looked so lifeless,
It was as if they're lifeless spirits,
Drifting away with the wind.

As I rise on my feet, I run
Forward.
All I want to do is fight,
Fight for the poor souls;
Who never got a chance to have their say.
So as I take my final shot,
My last words were:
'Goodbye world!'

Elizabeth P (13)
The Funwork School, London

Boom, Boom, Boom

I love listening to rapping,
and my fingers don't stop tapping.

My idol is Britney Spears,
I really wished she was here.

I hum while I listen to the music,
that's because I'm a cool chick.

The song goes boom, boom, boom;
cos it's my favourite tune.

I listen to the beat,
while I tap with my feet.

I dance to the beat of
boom, boom, boom.

Mariam A (12)
The Funwork School, London

Ode To Dad

I find it funny, how when I remember Mum
The most prominent trait I see in my head,
Is how she cried all the time,
How red her wrists were,
Why her eyes were always bruised.

I was only five years old, you'd always be drinking too much,
Did you ever quit? No, instead you'd just cuss
more every night, breaking everything in your sight.
And apparently, Mum was always in your eye.

I was five, and I wouldn't know why,
but every time I saw my mum cry,
It'd break my heart.

So it felt like my heart was broken
every day.

I guess I didn't realise at that age,
Why I felt like that.
You'd always come home, and when you
Sat down, she could barely stand up,
because you hurt her so much.
And then when you woke up,
You'd apologise as if that's all it took to cover up.

But you want to know what, Dad,
It takes a lot more than an apology to clean blood up.

I'm not sure why I decided to visit you behind bars,
You left me, mum, and my brain littered in scars.
I don't think I realised until I was thirteen, how far,
You'd taken it.

You know Mum always saw the best in you,
And when I was old enough I wanted her to leave you,
But she'd always say that she loved you too
Much.

And I always thought that was strange,
How could you love someone who
punched holes through doors,
or made you coil up on the floor,
Made your entire body,
And your entire mind,
Sore.

But because of you,
I started to associate,
Love with pain,

And you know what Dad, you made me insane.
You made me beat my own son, Dad,
Look what you've done!
My own wife's left me now, she's up and gone.

This is your fault Dad, and this goes out to you.
Because you were alone behind those bars,
Now I'm in with you too.

Marc French (16)
The Holy Cross School, New Malden

Dear Mother

Dear Mother,

I've gone away, just for a bit, but have no hope that I will return,
They don't approve of our Jewish faith, for the Christian religion they yearn.
I've gone away, just for a bit, but do not believe I will survive,
Maybe I will soon see you again, dead or perhaps alive.

I've gone away, just for a bit, please know that I love you so,
Although I fear the end is near I stay calm as my fate I don't know.
I've gone away, just for a bit, perhaps the camps aren't as they seem,
The inmates described it as nothing but hell, but maybe that just is a dream.

I've gone away, just for a bit, not to worry, this place is just fine,
Please convert to a Christian today, or you'll end up in firing line.
I've gone away, just for a bit, the horrors you will never find out,
I pray reception will be clear soon, so maybe then I can check out.

I've gone away, just for a bit, don't worry, I'll see you quite soon,
The sun shines not in the night-time, the comforting light is the moon.

I've gone away, just for a bit, my time will soon come to an end,
My ending is scheduled for Friday, please send my love to my friends.

I've gone away, just for a bit, I know that you'll join me today,
Meet me in the cavern at midnight, oh how I wish you could stay!
I've gone away, just for a bit, my executioner has a gun at my head,
He shoots with a bang, once then twice, and on the third one I am dead.

I've gone away, just for a bit, the casualties here are so great,
My time has come and so very sadly I have come to a similar fate.
I've gone away, just for a bit, when will these torture camps close?
The conditions here put a chill through your flesh, right from your head to your toes.

I've gone away, just for a bit, how will life ever go on?
Guiltless people, old and young, thanks to these actions are gone.
I've gone away, just for a bit, please fill the world with love,
I watch you and guide you every day, leaning on you from above.

I've gone away, just for a bit, please know I shall never come back,
The days pass rapidly, waiting for you, to search for the name on my plaque.
I've gone away, just for a bit, I sign this your beautiful child,
My greatest praise I send to you and I hope from this that you smiled.

I've gone away, just for a bit, I'll see you when you come,
In twenty years or maybe less, oh I do adore you, Mum.
I've gone away, just for a bit, I have to say goodbye,
I can't believe the end is here, oh my, oh my, oh my!

Rachel O'Connell (12)
The John Henry Newman Catholic School, Stevenage

Forgiveness Is Happiness

If you wouldn't forgive me,
I will never forgive you.
You will never be able to stop the tears
As you think of me or what you have done.
Don't let the disappointment rule you,
It's like giving yourself to the unhappiness
And I know you're better than that.
That's why I say sorry, before it's too late.
I know at first nobody believes the sorry
I didn't believe the sorry too
I thought sorry was a lie.
Sorry is just a word, I told myself,
It can't replace you or me.
But I was wrong,
For me it has changed,
Now I know sorry is forgiveness
Sorry means that people don't have anything to give you but would be willing to.
Sorry means that this person could not help it
They just knew that a devil controlled them.
I know that sorry is an irreplaceable thing.
Sorry is the entrance to a new world
A world that only you can enter, but you will need a friend
To help you enter it.

As hard as you may try, this world will never appear, you can't see it
But only feel as the sorry arrives.
Till after the sorry has been spoken out loud
The gates will open, to an astronomically, amazing new world!
You see arguments are needed for human beings
You will never be happy without them.
So see sorry says sweets and true things to you
Don't have a hard-hearted heart and don't be stubborn
Don't let this happen can't you see,
Every relationship you break
The nearer you are to your loneliness
I am human, that's why I can feel alone.
Some people enjoy the loneliness
But only those people do when they grow up without friends
In my opinion they are not human
But I believe that you are a human-being
And human-being just can't live without friend or family
Because if there's no one to die for,
There is no meaning of life
So don't hurt yourself.
Believe me, I'm saying it to protect you
You will not be proud of what you've done
Someday, you will regret it
But only to those who are fool,
They get tricked.

So forgive people and it will make you feel better too,
You will feel happier that you have had the chance to help and
This person will adore you.
Afterwards, I shall predict that, as a warning
When they are in need, give them your trust
And someday they will repay
Never forget
Friendship is much too valuable, more than money, diamond or crystals,
And you will have something, something that you will never have had
That you may not see, but feel
Your heart goes warm
Now wave goodbye to the loneliness
And always welcome your friend.
So now you understand that friendship is a gift, that everyone should have
When I heard those words coming out of my mouth, I was shocked because
even I didn't know what I was talking about,
But it doesn't matter, you only need to understand the importance
When you have done that you are a free and independent,
Independence is happiness.

Sarah Car (12)
The Kingston Academy, Kingston Upon Thames

The Clan

This man is the symbol to my clan
The man joined the clan
The leader asked for a battle plan
The man's plan started to drown in a watering can
Then he said, 'Face me man to man'
They fought and he beat the leader of this clan
The leader then created this man, as the symbol to his clan.

Christopher Liu (12)
The Kingston Academy, Kingston Upon Thames

Sui Generis

Everywhere, Sui Generis, everyone is
You, yourself are one of a kind
It's yours, mine, hers and his
The thoughts you think are in your mind.

A tree, rock, cloud or snowflake
Not two or three but one in all
There can only be one of its make
Thick or thin or short or tall
Life itself is your perception
No matter who we are, we're all allowed
Your friends, your family, every relation
Country, city, county or town
It all depends on your decision
Race, sexuality and religion.

Diversity is something that has no control
The suffragettes had the power to change
So skin, religion or gender means nothing at all
Martin Luther King had ideas to exchange
Not known by each other
Their ideas made the world accept
But like a sister or a brother
The ones who were different are now not left
No matter who you are we are all equal
There's no good, no insane, no same, no evil.

Books we have are different in ways
The subjects that we talk about can all be unique
But altogether they're all the same
Just let your thoughts run happily free
My poem came straight from my heart
When it comes to writing, it feels so right
To make sure that we are not apart
It helps me get to sleep at night
Knowing that my thoughts have been heard
Free to speak about what you like
Like a poet that has done spoken word
As if you've climbed over a mountain peak
Buzz, flitter, rustle and squeak
The sounds that are heard by us every week.

Now this stanza is all about me
I love flowers blooming with intense colour
The thing I like and love to see
Like the growth of your own little brother
The sun rising on the horizon
The essence of nature, that's all around
The silver moon smiling, unfrozen
The look, the smell, the colours, the sound
School is now a different subject
Even though, there's knowledge I will learn
Waking up is something that I object
But education will relieve me from future concern.

Sui generis is always there
Sui generis is why you care
Sui generis is near and far
Sui generis is who you are.

Nathan Joseph Dawkins (13)
The Kingston Academy, Kingston Upon Thames

The Power Of Past, Present And Future Tense

The past,
I lived it.
The present,
I'm living it.
The future,
Is beyond me.
The past can't be changed,
But can be forgotten.
As the present is in you,
And the future is beyond you.
Think only of the present,
The future shall think of itself
And the present dreams of the past.

Antonia Tyrer (11)
The St Leonards Academy, St. Leonards-On-Sea

Emotion

Happiness; like the feeling of a long, warm hug after a cold, harsh day of school,
Happiness; like the smell of a fresh apple pie, with a crisp, golden top,
Happiness; like the sight of a newborn pig squirming around, with its new-found love for life,
Happiness; like the sound of the kettle boiling ready for a delicious hot chocolate, with marshmallows melting and oozing on top,
Happiness; like the taste of refreshing watermelon on a hot summer's day, trickling down my throat,
Depression; like the feeling of sadness and loneliness usually hidden in the coldness of the school day,
Depression; like the smell of your favourite meal, burning to a crisp, black mess in the oven,
Depression; like the sight of a much-loved family member in severe pain that you can do nothing about,
Depression; like the sound of a crying baby, screaming for its mother, alone and desperate,
Depression; like the taste of a dead chicken wishing for life but being brutally murdered,
Love; like the feeling of something warm and fuzzy, nothing else is quite like it,
Love; like the smell of Christmas dinner fresh out of the oven, served delicately on the festively decorated table,
Love; like the sight of the most amazing person that you know, you want to spend the rest of your life with,
Love; like the sound of the loud wedding bells ringing on the most important day of your life,

Love; like the taste of chocolate chip cookies, melting and trickling down my throat,
Hate; like the feeling of all your worst enemies ganging up on you, ready to attack,
Hate; like the smell of blood and death mixed into one awful vile in the evil clutches of an insane professor that lives on the top of a mountain,
Hate; like the sight of an unwilling soldier, about to kill an innocent child,
Hate; like the sound of a gang of bullies screaming at the crying boy on the floor,
Hate; like the taste of poison boiling your blood and stripping you down to your last few moments,
Emotion; a mixed bag of good and evil, which do you like the sound of more?

Melody Forbes (11) & Isobel Jenner (12)
The St Leonards Academy, St. Leonards-On-Sea

Shadow

You were behind me all along,
You were singing an eerie, creepy song,
You were there behind every corner,
You were ready to pounce,
You were ready to pounce.

I felt as if someone was watching me,
I felt as if I wasn't quite free,
I felt like I had someone protecting me,
I felt as if I wasn't alone,
I felt as if I wasn't alone.

But I didn't really need protection,
But I didn't really need correction,
But I didn't need your hundred percent assistance,
But I didn't need you,
But I didn't need you.

Someone was behind me,
Someone made me want to flee,
Someone tried to make me feel uncomfortable,
Someone wanted me to go,
Someone wanted me to go.

That was you,
That was definitely you,
That was most definitely you,

You,
Yes you,
My shadow...

Libby Johnstone (11)
The St Leonards Academy, St. Leonards-On-Sea

YOUNG WRITERS INFORMATION

We hope you have enjoyed reading this book – and that you will continue to in the coming years.

If you're a young adult who enjoys reading and creative writing, or the parent of an enthusiastic poet or story writer, do visit our website **www.youngwriters.co.uk.** Here you will find free competitions, workshops and games, as well as recommended reads, a poetry glossary and our blog.

If you would like to order further copies of this book, or any of our other titles, then please give us a call or visit **www.youngwriters.co.uk.**

Young Writers
Remus House
Coltsfoot Drive
Peterborough
PE2 9BF
(01733) 890066
info@youngwriters.co.uk

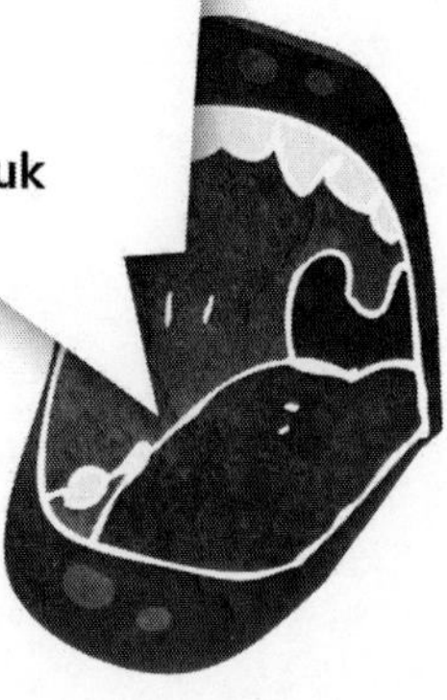